HARDPRESS.NET
HOME OF HARD-TO-FIND BOOKS

A Letter on Shakspeare's Authorship of the Two Noble Kinsmen; a Drama Commonly Ascribed to John Fletcher

by William Spalding

Address:
HardPress
8345 NW 66TH ST #2561
MIAMI FL 33166-2626
USA
Email: info@hardpress.net

A LETTER

SHAKSPEARE'S AUTHORSHIP

The Two Noble Kinsmen

Price 3s. 6d.

A LETTER

ON

SHAKSPEARE'S AUTHORSHIP

OF

The Two Noble Kinsmen;

A DRAMA COMMONLY ASCRIBED
TO JOHN FLETCHER.

EDINBURGH:
ADAM AND CHARLES BLACK;
AND LONGMAN, REES, ORME, BROWN, GREEN, AND LONGMAN,
LONDON.

M.DCCC.XXXIII.

Edinburgh :
Printed by A. Balfour and Co. Niddry Street.

A LETTER

ON

SHAKSPEARE'S AUTHORSHIP

OF

THE DRAMA ENTITLED

THE TWO NOBLE KINSMEN.

MY DEAR L——, We have met again, after an interval long enough to have made both of us graver than we were wont to be. A few of my rarely granted hours of leisure have lately been occupied in examining a question on which your taste and knowledge equally incline and qualify you to enter. Allow me to address to you the result of my inquiry, as a pledge of the gratification which has been afforded me by the renewal of our early intercourse.

Proud as SHAKSPEARE's countrymen are of his name, it is singular, though not unaccountable, that at this day our common list of his works should remain open to correction. Every one knows that some plays printed in his volumes have weak claims to that distinction; but, while the exclusion even of works certainly not his would now be a rash exercise of prerogative in any editor, it is a question of more interest, whether there may not be dramas not yet admitted among his collected works, which have a right to be there, and might be inserted without the danger attending the dismissal of any already put upon the list. A claim for admission has been set up in favour of Malone's six plays,* without any ground as to five of them, and

* Locrine—Sir John Oldcastle—Lord Cromwell—The London Prodigal—The Puritan—The Yorkshire Tragedy.

with very little to support it even for the sixth. Ireland's impostures are an anomaly in literary history: even the spell and sway of temporary fashion and universal opinion are causes scarcely adequate to account for the blindness of the eminent men who fell into the snare. The want of any external evidence in favour of the first fabrication, the Shakspeare papers, was overlooked; and the internal evidence, which was wholly against the genuineness, was unhesitatingly admitted as establishing it. The play of Vortigern had little more to support it than the previous imposition.

There are two cases, however, in which we have external presumptions to proceed from; for there are traditions traceable to Shakspeare's own time, or nearly so, of his having assisted in two plays, still known to us, but never placed among his works. The one, the Sejanus, in which Shakspeare is said to have assisted Jonson, was re-written by the latter himself, and published as it now stands among his writings, the part of the assistant poet having been entirely omitted; so that the question as to that play, a very doubtful question, is not important, and hardly even curious. But the other drama is in our hands as it came from the closets of the poets; and, if Shakspeare's partial authorship were established, ought to have a place among his works. It is, as you know, THE TWO NOBLE KINSMEN, printed among the works of Beaumont and Fletcher, and sometimes attributed to SHAKSPEARE and FLETCHER jointly. I have been able to satisfy myself that it is rightly so attributed, and hope to be able to prove to you, who are intimately conversant with Shakspeare, and familiar also with the writings of his supposed coadjutor, that there are good grounds for the opinion. The same conclusion has already been reached by others; but the discussion of the question cannot be needless so long as this fine drama continues excluded from the received list of Shakspeare's works; and while there is reason to believe that there are many discerning students and zealous admirers of the poet, to whom it is known only by name. The beauty of the work itself will make much of the investigation delightful to you, even though my argument on it may seem feeble and stale.

The proof is, of course, two-fold; the first branch emerging from any records or memorials which throw light on the subject from without, the second from a consideration of the work itself, and a comparison of its qualities with those of Shakspeare or Fletcher. You will keep in mind, that it has not been doubted, and may be assumed, that Fletcher had a share in the work; the only question is,—Whether Shakspeare wrote any part of it, and what parts, if any?

The Historical Evidence claims our attention in the first instance; but in no question of literary genuineness is this the sort of proof which yields the surest grounds of conviction. Such questions arise only under circumstances in which the external proof on either side is very weak, and the internal evidence has therefore to be continually resorted to for supplying the defects of the external. It is true, that a complete proof of a work having been actually written by a particular person, destroys any contrary presumption from intrinsic marks; and, in like manner, when a train of evidence is deduced, shewing it to be impossible that a work could have been written by a certain author, no internal likeness to other works of his can in the least weaken the negative conclusion. In either case, however, the historical evidence must be incontrovertible before it can exclude examination of the internal; and the two cases are by no means equally frequent. It scarcely ever happens that there is external evidence weighty enough to establish certainly, of itself, an individual's authorship of a particular work; but the external proof that his authorship was impossible may often be convincing and perfect, from an examination of dates, or the like. Since, therefore, external evidence against authorship admits of completeness, we are entitled, when such evidence exclusively is founded on, to demand that it shall be complete. Where by the very narrowest step it falls short of a demonstration of absolute impossibility, the internal evidence cannot be refused admittance in contravention of it, and comes in with far greater force than that of the other. There may be cases where authorship can be made out to the highest degree, at least, of probability, by strong internal evidence coming in aid of an external proof equally balanced for and against; and even where the extrinsic proof is of itself sufficient to infer improbability, internal marks may be so decided the opposite way, as to render the question absolutely doubtful, or to occasion a leaning towards the affirmative side. These principles point out the internal evidence as the true ground on which my cause must be contested; but it was not necessary to follow them out to their full extent; for I can shew you, that the external facts which we have here, few as they are, raise a presumption in favour of Shakspeare's authorship, as strong as exists in cases of more practical importance, where its effect has never been questioned.

The fact from which the maintainers of Shakspeare's share in this drama have to set out, is the first printing of it, which took place in 1634. In the title-page of this first edition,* the play is stated to be the joint work of Shakspeare and Fletcher. It is needless to enumerate categorically the doubts which have been thrown, chiefly by the acute and perverse Steevens, on the credit due to this assertion; for a few observations will shew that they have by no means an overwhelming force, while there are contrary presumptions far more than sufficient to weigh them down. The edition was not published till eighteen years after Shakspeare's death, and nine years after Fletcher's; but any suspicion which might arise from the length of this interval, as giving an opportunity for imposture, is at once removed by one consideration, which is almost an unanswerable argument in favour of the assertion on the title-page, and in contravention of this or any other doubts. There was no motive for falsely stating Shakspeare's authorship, because no end would have been gained by it; for it is a fact admitting of the fullest proof, that, even so recently after Shakspeare's death as 1634, he had fallen much into neglect. Fletcher had become far more popular, and his name in the title-page would have been a surer passport to public favour than Shakspeare's. If either of the names was to be

* "The Two Noble Kinsmen: presented at the Blackfriers, by the Kings Majesties servants, with great Applause: written by the memorable Worthies of their Time, Mr. John Fletcher and Mr. William Shakspeare, Gent. Printed at London by Tho. Cotes, for John Watersone; and are to be sold at the signe of the Crowne, in Pauls Church-yard: 1634."

fabricated, Fletcher's, (which stands foremost in the title-page as printed,) was the more likely of the two to have been preferred. It appears then that the time when the publisher's assertion of Shakspeare's authorship was made, gives it a right to more confidence than it could have deserved if it had been advanced earlier. If the work had been printed during the poet's life and the height of his popularity, its title-page would have been no evidence at all. And when the assertion is freed from the suspicion of designed imposture, the truth of it is confirmed by its stating the play to have been acted by the king's servants, and at the Blackfriars. It was that company which had been Shakspeare's, the Globe and Blackfriars were the two theatres at which they played, and at one or the other of these houses all his acknowledged works seem to have been brought out. The fact of the play not having been printed sooner, is accounted for by the dramatic arrangements and practice of the time: the first collected edition of Shakspeare's works, only eleven years earlier than the printing of this play, contained about twenty plays of his not printed during his life; and the long interval is a reason also why the printer and publisher are different persons from any who were concerned in Shakspeare's other works. The hyperbolical phraseology of the title-page is quite in the taste of the day, and is exceeded by the quarto editions of some of Shakspeare's admitted works.

Was the alleged co-operation then in itself likely to have taken place? It was. Such partnerships were very generally formed by the dramatists of that time; both the poets were likely enough to have projected some union of the kind, and to have chosen each other as the parties to it. Although Shakspeare seems to have followed this custom less frequently than most of his contemporaries, we have reason to think that he did not wholly refrain from it; and his favourite plan of altering plays previously written by others, is a near approach to it. As to Fletcher, his name is connected in every mind with that of Beaumont, and the memorable and melancholy letter of the three players,* proves him to have coalesced with other writers even during that poet's short

* Gifford's Massinger, vol. i. p. xv.

life. This is of some consequence, because, if the two poets wrote at the same time, it would seem that they must have done so previously to Beaumont's death; for Shakspeare lived only one year longer than Beaumont, and is believed to have spent that year in the country. There is no proof that the drama before us was not written before Beaumont's death, (1615) and it is only certain that its era was later than 1594. After the loss of his friend, Fletcher is said to have been repeatedly assisted by Massinger: he joined in one play with Jonson and Middleton, and in another with Rowley. His superior rank (he was the son of a bishop) has been gravely mentioned as discrediting his connexion with Shakspeare; but the same objection applies with infinitely greater force to his known co-operation with Field, Daborne, and the others just named; and the idea is founded on radically wrong notions of the temper of that age. There is scarcely more substance in a doubt raised from the frequency with which Shakspeare is burlesqued by Beaumont and Fletcher. Those satirical flings could have been no reason why Fletcher should be unwilling to coalesce with Shakspeare, because they indicate no ill feeling towards him. They were practised by all the dramatic writers at the expense of each other; Shakspeare himself is a parodist, and indulges in those quips frequently, not against such writers only as the author of the Spanish Tragedy, but against Peele and even Marlowe, his own fathers in the drama, and both dead before he vented the jests, which he never would have uttered had he attached to them any degree of malice. And therefore also Fletcher's sarcasms cannot have disinclined Shakspeare to the coalition, especially as his personal character made it very unlikely that he should have taken up any such grudge as a testy person might have conceived from some of the more severe.

But the circumstance on which most stress has been laid as disproving Shakspeare's share in the drama in question, is this. While the first edition of it was not printed till 1634, two editions of Shakspeare's collected works had been published between the time of his death (1616) and that year, in neither of which this play appears; and it is said that its omission in the first folio (1623), in particular, is fatal to its claim, since Heminge and

Condell, who edited that collection, were Shakspeare's fellow-actors and the executors of his will, and must be presumed to have known perfectly what works were and what were not his. I have put this objection as strongly as it can be put, and at first sight it is startling; but those who have most bibliographical knowledge of Shakspeare's works are best aware that much of its force is only apparent. The omission in the second folio (1632) should not have been founded on; for that edition is nothing but a reprint of the contents of the first; and it is only the want of the play in this latter that we have to consider. Now, you know well, that in taking some objections to the authority of the First Folio, I shall only echo the opinions of Shakspeare's most judicious critics. It was a speculation on the part of the editors for their own advantage, either solely or in conjunction with any others, who, as holders of shares in the Globe Theatre, had an interest in the plays: for it was to the theatre, you will remark, and not to Shakspeare or his heirs personally, that the manuscripts belonged. The edition shews distinctly, that profit was its aim more than faithfulness to the memory of the poet, in the correctness either of his text or of the list of his works. Even the style of the preface excites suspicions which the work itself verifies. One object of it was to put down editions of about fifteen separate plays of Shakspeare's, previously printed in quarto, which, though in most respects more accurate than their successors, had evidently been taken from stolen copies: the preface of the folio, accordingly, strives to throw discredit on these quartos, while the text, usually close in its adherence to them, falls into errors where it quits them, and omits many very fine passages which they give, and which the modern editors have been enabled by their assistance to restore.

Here it is, however, of more consequence to notice, that the authority of the Table of Contents of the Folio is worse than weak. The editors profess to give all Shakspeare's works, and none which are not his: we know that they have fulfilled neither the one pledge nor the other. There is no doubt but they could at least have enumerated Shakspeare's works correctly: but their knowledge and their design of profit did not suit each other. They have admitted, for plain reasons, two plays which are not Shakspeare's. Their edition contains about twenty plays never before printed; it was evidently their interest to enlarge this part of their list as far as they safely could. The pretended First Part of Henry VI., in which Shakspeare may perhaps have written a single scene,* but certainly not twenty lines besides, had not been printed, and could be plausibly inserted; it does not seem that they could have had any other reasons for giving it a place. The Tragedy of the Shambles, which we call Titus Andronicus, if it had been printed at all, had been so only once, and that thirty years before; therefore it likewise was a novelty, and a pretext was easily found for its admission. The editors then were unscrupulous and unfair as to the works which they inserted: professing to give a full collection, they were no less so as to those which they did not insert. Troilus and Cressida, an unpleasing drama, contains many passages of the highest spirit and poetical richness, and the bad in it, as well as the good, is perfectly characteristic of Shakspeare; it is unquestionably his. It does not appear in Heminge and Condell's table of contents, and is only found appended, like a separate work, to some copies of their edition. Its pages are not even numbered along with the rest of the volume; and if the first editors were the persons who printed it, it was clearly after the remainder of the work. If they did print it, their manner of doing so shews their carelessness of truth more strongly than if they had omitted it altogether. They first make up their list and state it as a full one without that play, which they apparently had been unable to obtain; they then procure access to the manuscript, print the play, and insert it in the awkward way in which it stands, and thus virtually confess that the assertion in their preface, made in reference to their table of contents, was untrue. At any rate, a part of their impression was circulated without this play. Pericles also is wholly omitted by those editors; it appears for the first time in the third folio, (1666), an edition of no value, and its genuineness rests much on the internal proofs, which

* Act II. Scene 4. The plucking of the roses.

are quite sufficient to establish it. It is an irregular and imperfect play, older in form than any of Shakspeare's; but it has clearly been augmented by many passages written by him, and therefore had a right to be inserted by the first editors, upon their own principles. These two plays then being certainly Shakspeare's, no matter whether his best or his worst, and his editors being so situated that they must have known the fact, their edition is allowed to appear as a complete collection of Shakspeare's works, although its contents include neither of the two. They probably were unable to procure copies; but they were not the less bound to have acknowledged in their preface, that these or any other plays which they knew to be Shakspeare's, were necessary for making up a complete collection. It in no view suited their purposes to make such a statement; and it was not made. In short, the whole conduct of these editors inspires distrust, but their unacknowledged omission of those two plays deprives them of all claim to our confidence. The effect of that omission, in reference to any play which can be brought forward as Shakspeare's, is just this, that the want of the drama in their edition is of itself no proof whatever that Shakspeare was not the author of it, and leaves the question, whether he was or was not, perfectly open for decision on other evidence. It leaves the inquiry before us precisely in that situation. Why Heminge and Condell could not procure the manuscripts of Troilus, Pericles, or the Two Noble Kinsmen, I am not bound to shew. As to the last, Fletcher may have retained a partial or entire right of property in it, and was alive at the publication of their edition. Difficulties at least as great attach to the question as to the other two rejected plays, in which the strength of the other proofs has long been admitted as counterbalancing them. But the argument serves my purpose without any theory on the subject. The state of it entitles me, as I conceive, to throw the First Folio entirely out of view, as being no evidence one way or the other.

Laying the folio aside then, I think I have shewn that, in the most unfavourable view, no doubts which other circumstances can throw on the assertion made in the title-page of the first edition of the Two Noble Kinsmen, are of such strength as to render the truth of it improbable. Strong internal evidence therefore will, in any view, establish Shakspeare's claim. But, if the consideration first suggested be well-founded, (as I have no doubt it is,) namely, that the statement of the publisher was disinterested, there arises a very strong external presumption of the truth of his assertion, which will enable us to proceed to the examination of the internal marks with a prepossession in favour of Shakspeare's authorship.

As I wish to make you a convert to the affirmative opinion, it may be wise to acquaint you that you will not be alone in it, if you shall finally see reason to embrace it. Shakspeare, you know, suffered a long eclipse, which left him in obscurity till the beginning of last century, when he reappeared surrounded by his annotators, a class of men who have followed a narrow track, but yet are greater benefactors to us than we are ready to acknowledge. The commentators have given little attention to the question before us ; but some of the best of them have declared incidentally for Shakspeare's claim, and though even the editors who have professed this belief have not inserted the work as his, this is only one among many evil results of the slavish system to which they all adhere. We have with us Pope, Warburton, and above all, Farmer, a man of fine discernment, and a most cautious sifter of evidence. The subject has more recently been treated shortly by a celebrated foreign critic, the enthusiastic and eloquent Schlegel,* who comes to a conclusion decidedly favourable to Shakspeare.

There still lies before us the principal part of our task, that of applying to the presumption resulting from the external proof, (whatever the amount of that may be,) the decisive test of the

* Lectures on Dramatic Art and Literature. It would ill become me to carp at an author whom I have expressly to thank for much assistance in this inquiry, and to whom I am perhaps indebted for more than my recollection suggests. But it must be owned, that M. Schlegel's opinion loses somewhat of its weight from the fact, that he also advocates Shakspeare's authorship of some of Malone's plays, a decision in which it is neither desirable nor likely that the poet's countrymen should acquiesce.

Internal Evidence. Do you doubt the efficacy of this supposed crucial experiment? It is true that internal similarities form almost a valueless test when applied to inferior writers; because in them the distinctive marks are too weak to be easily traced. But, in the first place, great authors have in their very greatness the pledge of something peculiar which shall identify their works, and consequently the test is usually satisfactory in its application to them; and, secondly and particularly, Shakspeare is, of all writers that have existed, that one to whose alleged works such a test can be most confidently administered; because he is not only strikingly peculiar in those qualities which discriminate him from other poets, but his writings also possess singularities different from and opposite to the usual character of poetry itself.

I cannot proceed with you to the work itself, till I have reminded you of some distinctive differences between the two writers whose claims we are to adjust, the recollection of which will be indispensible to us in considering the details of the drama. We shall then enter on that detailed examination, keeping those distinctions in mind, and attempting to apply them to individual passages; and, when all the scenes of the play have thus passed successively before us, we shall be able to look back on it as a whole, and investigate its general qualities.

The first difference which may be pointed out between Shakspeare and Fletcher, is that of their versification. You have learned from a study of the poets themselves in what that difference consists. Shakspeare's versification is broken and full of pauses, he is sparing of double terminations to his verses, and has a marked fondness for ending speeches or scenes with hemistiches. Fletcher's rhythm is of a newer and smoother cast, often keeping the lines distinct and without breaks through whole speeches, abounding in double endings, and very seldom leaving a line incomplete at the end of a sentence or scene.* And the opposite taste of the two poets in their choice and arrangement

* Weber's Beaumont and Fletcher, vol. xiii., and Lamb, as there quoted.

of words, gives an opposite character to the whole modulation of their verses. Fletcher's is sweet and flowing, and peculiarly fitted either for declamation or the softness of sorrow: Shakspeare's ear is tuned to the stateliest solemnity of thought, or the abruptness and vehemence of passion. The present drama exhibits in whole scenes the qualities of Shakspeare's versification; and there are other scenes which are marked by those of Fletcher's; the difference is one reason for separating the authorship.

You will notice in this play many instances of Shakspeare's favourite images, and of his very words. Is this a proof of the play having been his work, or does it only indicate imitation? In Shakspeare's case such resemblance, taken by itself, can operate neither way. Shakspeare is a mannerist in style. He knew this himself, and what he says of his minor poems, is equally true of his dramatic language: he "keeps invention in a noted weed;"* and almost every word or combination of words is so marked in its character that its author is known at a glance. But not only is his style so peculiar in its general qualities, as scarcely to admit of being mistaken; not only is it deficient in variety of structure, but it is in a particular degree characterised by a frequent recurrence of the same images often clothed in identically the same words. You are quite aware of this, and those who are not may be convinced of it by opening any page of the annotated editions. So far, then, this play is only like Shakspeare's acknowledged works. It is true, that one who wished to write a play in Shakspeare's manner, would probably have repeated his images and words as they are repeated here; but Shakspeare would certainly have imitated himself quite as often. The resemblance could be founded on as indicating imitation only in conjunction with other circumstances of dissimilarity or inferiority to his genuine writings; and where, as in the present case, there seems to be reason for asserting that the accompanying circumstances point the work out as an original composition of his, this very likeness and repetition becomes strong argument in support of those concomitant indications.

* Sonnet 76.

Such repetition is more or less common in all the play-writers of that age. The number of their works, the quickness with which they were written, and the carelessness which circumstances induced as to their elaboration or final correction, all aided in giving rise to this. But all are not equally chargeable with it; Beaumont and Fletcher less than most, Massinger to an extent far beyond Shakspeare, and vying with the common-places of Euripides. May not the professional habits of Shakspeare and Massinger as actors have had some effect in producing this, by imprinting their own works in their memories with unusual strength? Fletcher and his associate were free from that risk.

It would not be easy to give a systematic account of those qualities which combine to constitute Shakspeare's singularity of style. Some of them lie at the very surface, others are found only on a deeper search, and a few there are which depend on evanescent relations, instinctively perceptible to the congenial poetical sense, but extremely difficult of abstract prose definition. Several qualities also, which we are apt to think exclusively his, (such, for instance, as his looseness of construction,) are discovered on examination to be common to him with the other dramatic writers of his age. Such qualities can give no assistance in an inquiry like ours, and may be left wholly out of view. But I think the distinctions which I can specify between him and Fletcher are quite enough, and applicable with sufficient closeness to this drama, for making out the point which I wish to prove.

No one is ignorant that Shakspeare is concise, that this quality makes him always energetic and often most impressive, but that it also gives birth to much obscurity. He shews a constant wish to deliver thought, fancy, and feeling, in the fewest words possible. Even his images are brief; they are continual, and they crowd and confuse one another; the well-springs of his imagination boil up every moment, and the readiness with which they throw up their golden sands, makes him careless of fitly using the wealth thus profusely rendered. He abounds in hinted descriptions, in sketches of imagery, in glimpses of illustration, in abrupt and vanishing snatches of fancy. But the merest hint that he gives is of force enough to shew that the image was fully present with him: if he fails to bring it as distinctly before us, it is either from the haste with which he passes to another, or from the eagerness induced by the very force and quickness with which he has conceived the former. It has been said of Milton that language sunk under him, and it is true of him in one sense, but of Shakspeare in two. Shakspeare's strength of conception, to which, not less than to Milton's, existing language was inadequate, compelled him either to use old words in unusual meanings, or to coin new words for himself.* But his mind had another quality powerful over his style, which Milton's wanted. Milton's conception was comparatively slow, and allowed him time for deliberate expression: Shakspeare's was rapid to excess, and hurried his words after it. When a truth presented itself to his mind, all its qualities burst in upon him at once, and his instantaneousness of conception could be represented only by words as brief and quick as thought itself. This cause operates with the greatest force on his passages of reflection; for if his images are often brief, his apophthegms are brief a thousand times oftener: his quickness of ideas seems to have been stimulated to an extraordinary degree by the contemplation of general truths. And everywhere his incessant activity and quickness, both of intellect and fancy, engage him in a continual struggle with speech; it is a sluggish slave which he would force to bear a burden beyond its strength, a weary courser which he would urge at a speed to which it is unequal. He fails only from insufficiency in his puny instrument; not because his conception is indistinct, but because it is too full, energetic, and rapid, to receive adequate expression. It is excess of strength which hurts, not weakness which incapacitates; he is injured by the undue prevalence of the good principle, not by its defect. The obscurity of other writers is often the mistiness of the evening twilight sinking into night; his is the fitful dimness of the dawn, contending with the retiring darkness, and striving to break out

* There are numerous instances of both these effects in the play before us. "*Counter-reflect,* (a noun;) *meditance; couch* and *corslet* (used as verbs); *operance; appointment,* for military accoutrements; *globy eyes; scurril; disroot; dis-seat,*" &c. *Weber.*

into open day. Scarcely any writer of Shakspeare's class, or of any other, comes near him either in the faults or the grandeur which are the alternate results of this tendency of mind; but none is more utterly unlike him than the poet to whom, some would say, we must attribute passages in this play so singularly like Shakspeare. Fletcher is diffuse both in his leading thoughts and in his illustrations. His intellect did not present truth to him with the instant conviction which it poured on Shakspeare, and his fancy did not force imagery on him with a profusion which might have tempted him to weave its different suggestions into inconsistent forms; he expresses thought deliberately and with amplification; he paints his illustrative pictures with a careful hand and by repeated touches; his style has a pleasing and delicate air which is any thing but vigorous, and often reaches the verge of feebleness. Take a passage or two from the work before us, and do you say, who know Fletcher, whether they be his or the work of a stronger hand.

He only attributes
The faculties of other instruments
To his own nerves and act; commands men's service,
And what they gain in't, boot and glory too.
* * * What man
Thirds his own worth, (the case is each of ours,)
When that his action's dregged with mind assured
'Tis bad he goes about?

Act I. Scene 2.

Dowagers, take hands:
Let us be widows to our woes: Delay
Commends us to a famishing hope.

Act I. Scene 1.

I do not quote these lines for praise. The meaning of the last quotation in particular is obscure when it stands alone, and not too clear even when it is read in the scene. But I ask you, whether the oracular brevity of each of the sentences is not perfectly in the manner of Shakspeare. A fragment from another beautiful address in the first scene is equally characteristic and less faulty.

Honoured Hippolita,
Most dreaded Amazonian, that hast slain
The scythe-tusked boar; that, with thy arm as strong
As it is white, wast near to make the male
To thy sex captive, but that this thy lord
(*Born to uphold creation in that honour*
First Nature styled it in) shrunk thee into
The bound thou wast o'erflowing, at once subduing
Thy force and thy affection;—Soldieress!
That equally canst poise sternness with pity;—
Who now, I know, hast much more power o'er him
Than e'er he had on thee;—*who owest his strength*
And his love too, who is a servant to
The tenor of thy speech! * * *

Is this like Fletcher? I think not. It is unlike him in versification and in the tone of thought, and you will here particularly notice that it is unlike him in abruptness and brevity. It is like Shakspeare in all these particulars.

I have said that Shakspeare, often obscure, is scarcely ever vague; that he may fail to express all he wishes, but almost always gives distinctly the part which he is able to convey. Fletcher is not only slow in his ideas, but often vague and deficient in precision. The following lines are taken from a scene in the play under our notice, which clearly is not Shakspeare's. I would direct your attention, not to the remoteness of the last conceit, but to the want of distinctness in grasping images, and the inability to see fully either their picturesque or their poetical relations.

Arcite. We were not bred to talk, man: when we are armed,
And both upon our guards, then *let our fury,*
Like meeting of two tides, fly strongly from us.
* * * * *
Palamon. Methinks this armour's very like that, Arcite,
Thou worest that day the three kings fell, but lighter.
Arc. That was a very good one; and that day,
I well remember, you out-did me, cousin:
* * When I saw you charge first,
Methought I heard a dreadful clap of thunder
Break from the troop.
Pal. *But still before that flew*
The lightning of your valour.

Act III. Scene 6.

Shakspeare's style, as every one knows, is metaphorical to excess. His imagination is always active, but he seldom pauses to indulge it by lengthened description. I shall hereafter have occasion to direct your observation to the sobriety with which he preserves imagination in its proper station, as only the minister and interpreter of thought; but what I wish now to say is, that in him the two powers operate simultaneously. He goes on thinking vigorously, while his imagination scatters her inexhaustible treasures like flowers on the current of his meditations. His constant aim is the expression of facts, passions, or opinions; and his intellect is constantly occupied in the investigation of such; but the mind acts with ease in its lofty vocation, and the beautiful and the grand rise up voluntarily to do him homage. He never indeed consents to express those poetical ideas by themselves; but he shows that he felt their import and their legitimate use, by wedding them to the thoughts in which they originated. The truths which he taught received magnificence and amenity from the illustrative forms; and the poetical images were elevated into a higher sphere of associations by the dignity of the principles which they were applied to adorn. Something like this is always the true function of the imagination in poetry, and dramatic poetry in particular, and it is also the test which tries the presence of the faculty; metaphor indicates its strength, and simile its weakness. Nothing can be more different from this, or farther inferior to it, than the style of a poet who turns aside in search of description, and indulges in simile preferably to the brevity of metaphor; to whom perhaps a poetical picture originally suggested itself as the decoration of a striking thought, but who allowed himself to be captivated by the beauty of the suggested image, till he forgot the thought which had given it birth, and on its connexion with which its highest excellence depended. Such was Fletcher, whose style is poor in metaphor. His descriptions are sometimes beautifully romantic; but even then the effect of the whole is often picturesque rather than poetically touching; and it is evident that lengthened description can still less frequently be dramatic. In his descriptions, it is observable that the poetieal relations introduced in illustration are usually few, the character of the leading subject being relied on for producing the poetical effect. Fletcher's longest descriptions are but elegant outlines; Shakspeare's briefest metaphors are often finished paintings. Where Shakspeare is guilty of detailed description, he is very often laboured, cold, and involved; but his illustrative ideas are invariably copious, and it is often their superfluity which chiefly tends to mar the general effect. In the play that you are to examine, you will find a profusion of metaphor, which is undoubtedly the offspring of a different mind from Fletcher's; and both its excellence and its peculiarity of character seem to me to stamp it as Shakspeare's. I think the following passage cannot be mistaken, though the beginning is difficult, and the text perhaps incorrect.

> They two have *cabined*
> In many as dangerous, as poor a corner—
> Peril and want contending, they have *skiffed*
> Torrents whose raging *tyranny* and *power*
> I' the least of these was dreadful; and they have
> Fought out together where *Death's self* was *lodged*,
> Yet FATE hath BROUGHT THEM OFF. Their *knot* of love,
> Tied, *weaved*, ENTANGLED, with so true, so long,
> And with a *finger* of so deep a cunning,
> May be *outworn*, never *undone*. I think
> Theseus cannot be *umpire* to himself,
> *Cleaving his conscience into twain*, and doing
> Each side like justice, which he loves best.
>
> *Act I. Scene 3.*

The play throughout will give you metaphors, like Shakspeare's in their frequency, like his in their tone and character, and like his in their occasional obscurity and blending together.

We have been looking to Shakspeare's imagery. You will meet with classical images in The Two Noble Kinsmen. Do not allow any ill-applied notion of his want of learning to convert this into an argument against his authorship. You will recollect, that an attachment of this sort is very perceptible in Shakspeare's dramas, and pervades the whole thread of his youthful poems. It is indeed a prominent quality in the school of poetry, which prevailed during the earlier part of his life, perhaps during the whole of it. In his early days, the study of

Grecian and Latin literature in England may be said to have only commenced, and the scenery and figures of the classical mythology broke on the view of the student with all the force of novelty. All the literature of that period is tinged with classicism to a degree which in our satiated times is apt to seem pedantic. It infected writers of all kinds and classes: translations were multiplied, and a familiarity with classical tales and history was sought after or affected even by those who had no access to the original language. Shakspeare clearly stood in this latter predicament, his knowledge of Latin certainly not exceeding that of a schoolboy: but the translated classics enabled him to acquire the facts, and he shared the taste of the age to its full extent. His admiration of the classical writers is vouched by the subjects and execution of his early poems, by numerous allusions in his dramas, particularly his histories, by the subjects chosen for some of his plays, by one or two imitations of the translated Latin poets,* and by many exotic forms in his language, derived from the same secondary source. Correct tameness is the usual character of classical allusion in authors well versed in classical studies. Even Milton, who has drawn the most exquisite images of this kind, has sometimes remembered only, where he should have invented: and Fletcher, whom we have especially to consider, is no exception to the rule; his many classical illustrations are invariably cold and poor. Shakspeare's mythological images have something singular in them. They are incorrect as transcripts of the originals, but admirable if examined without such reference; they are highly coloured paintings whose subjects are taken from the simplicity of some antique statue. The Venus and Adonis has some fine and some overcharged pictures thus formed from the hints which he derived from his books.† He received the mythological images but imperfectly, and his fancy was stimulated without being

* Farmer's Essay on the Learning of Shakspeare.

† A singularly rich and energetic piece of colouring in this sort is near the beginning of the poem, commencing,

I have been wooed, as I entreat thee now,
Even by the stern and direful God of War—

and extending through three stanzas.

clogged. He stood but at the entrance of those visionary forests, within whose glades the heroes and divinities of ancient faith reposed; he looked through a glimmering and uncertain light, and caught only glimpses of the sanctity of that world of wonders: and it was with an imagination heated by the flame of mystery and partial ignorance that he turned away from the scene so imperfectly revealed, to brood on the beauty of its broken contours, and allow fancy to create magnificence richer than memory ever saw. The occurrence of classical allusions here, therefore, affords no reason for doubting his authorship even of those passages in which they are found: and if we could trace any of his singularities in the images which we have, the argument in his favour would be strengthened by these. Most of the allusions are too slightly sketched to permit this; but one or two are like him in their unfaithfulness. We have "Mars' drum" in the Venus and Adonis; and here beauty is described as able to make him spurn it: the altar of the same deity is alluded to as the scene of a Grecian marriage. The "Nemean lion's hide" is here, as his nerve in Hamlet. But the most characteristic use of this sort of imagery is in the prayer in the first scene of the Fifth Act. The whole tenor of the language, the solemnity and majesty of the tone of thought, the piling up of the heap of metaphors and images, and the boldness and admirable originality of their conception, all these are Shakspeare's; and the fact of this accumulation of feeling, thought, and imagination being employed to create out of a fragmentary classical outline a picture both new in its features and gorgeously magnificent in its filling up, is strongly indicative of his hand, and strikingly resembles his mode of dealing with such subjects elsewhere.

You will be furnished with a rule to guide your decision on many passages of the drama otherwise doubtful, by having your notice slightly directed to what will fall more properly under our consideration when we look back on the general scope of the play,—I mean Shakspeare's prevailing tendency to reflection. The presence of a spirit of active and inquiring thought through every page of his writings is too evident to require any proof. It is exerted on every object which comes under his notice: it is serious when its theme is lofty, and when the subject is familiar it is contented to be shrewd. He has impressed no other of his own mental qualities on all his characters: this quality colours every one of them. It is one to which poetry is apt to give a very subordinate place: and, in most poets, fancy is the predominating power; because, immeasurably as that faculty in them is beneath its unequalled warmth in Shakspeare, yet intellect in them is comparatively even weaker. With inferior poets, particularly the dramatic, inflation of feeling and profusion of imagery are the alternate disguises which conceal poverty of thought. Fletcher is a poet of much and sterling merit; but his fund of thought is small indeed when placed beside Shakspeare's. He has, indeed, very little of Shakspeare's practical, searching, worldly wisdom, and none of that solemnity of thought with which he penetrates into his loftier themes of reflection. This quality in Shakspeare is usually relieved by poetical decoration: Imagination is active powerfully and unceasingly, but she is rebuked by the presence of a mightier influence; she is but the handmaid of the active and piercing Understanding; and the images which are her offspring serve but as the breeze to the river, which stirs and ripples its surface, but is not the power which impels its waters to the sea. As you go through this drama, you will not only find a sobriety of tone pervading the more important parts of it, but activity of intellect constantly exerted. But what demands particular notice is, the mass of general truths, of practical, moral, or philosophical maxims, which, issuing from this reflective turn of mind, are scattered through Shakspeare's writings as thick as the stars in heaven. The occurrence of them is characteristic of his temper of mind, and there is something marked in the manner of the adages themselves. They are often solemn, usually grave, but always pointed, compressed, and energetic;—they vary in subject, from familiar facts and rules for social life to the enunciation of philosophical truths and the exposition of moral duty. You will meet with them in this drama in all their shapes and in every page.

Shakspeare's reach and comprehension of thought is as remarkable as its activity, while Fletcher's is by no means great, and in this respect Massinger comes much nearer to him. The simplest fact has many dependent qualities, and may be related by men of different degrees of intellect with circumstances differing infinitely, a confined mind seeing only its plainest qualities, while a stronger one grasps and combines many distant relations. Shakspeare's love of brevity would not have produced obscurity nearly so often, had it not been aided by his width of mental vision. There are many passages in the play before us which seem to emanate from a mind of more comprehension than Fletcher's. Look at the following lines. The idea to be expressed was a very simple one. Hippolita is entreating her husband to leave her, and depart to succour the distressed ladies who kneel at her feet and his; and she wishes to say, that though, as a bride, she was loth to lose her husband's presence, yet she felt that she should act blameably if she detained him. Fletcher would have expressed no idea beyond that; but on it alone he would have employed six lines and two or three comparisons. Hear how many cognate ideas present themselves to Shakspeare's mind in expressing the thought. The passage is obscure, but not the less like Shakspeare on that account.

> Though much unlikely
> I should be so transported, *as much sorry*
> *I should be such a suitor;* yet I think,
> Did I not, by the abstaining of my joy,
> *Which breeds a deeper longing,* cure the surfeit
> *That craves a present medicine,* I should pluck
> All ladies' scandal on me.
>
> *Act I. Scene* 1.

It would be well if Shakspeare's continual inclination to thought gave rise to no worse faults than occasional obscurity. It was not to be hoped that it should not produce others. His tone of thinking could not be always high and serious; and even when it flowed in a lofty channel, its uninterrupted stream could not always be pure. His judgment often fails to perform its part, and he is guilty of conceit and quibble, not merely in his comic vein, but in his most deeply tragical situations. He has indeed one powerful excuse; he had universal example in both respects to justify or betray him. But he has likewise another plea, that his constant activity of mind, and the wideness of its province, exposed him to peculiar risks. A mind always in action must sometimes act wrongly; and the constant exercise of the creative powers of the mind dulls the edge of the corrective. It was not strange that he who was unwearied in tracing the manifestations of that spirit of likeness which pervades nature, should often mistake a resemblance in name for a community of essence,—that he whose mind was sensible to the most delicate differences, should sometimes fancy he saw distinction where there was none;—it was not strange, however much to be regretted, that he who left the smooth green slopes of fancy to clamber among the craggy steeps of thought, should often stumble in his dizzy track, either in looking up to the perilous heights above, or downwards on the morning landscape beneath him. While the most glaring errors of the tropical Euphues are strained allegorical conceits, Shakspeare's fault is oftener the devising of subtle and unreal distinctions, or the ringing of fantastical changes upon words. Lily's error was one merely of taste, Shakspeare's was one of the judgment, and the heavier of the two, but still the error of a stronger mind than the other; for the judgment cannot act till the understanding has given it materials to work upon, and those fanciful writers who do not reflect at all are in no danger of reflecting wrongly. Shakspeare's evil genius triumphs when it tempts him to a pun—it enjoys a less complete but more frequent victory in suggesting an antithesis; but it often happens that this dangerous turn of mind does not carry him so far as to be of evil consequence. It aids his quickness and directness of mental view, in giving to his style a pointed epigrammatic terseness which is quite its own, and a frequent weight and effect which no other equals. Where, however, this antithetic tendency is allowed to approach the serious scenes, it throws over them an icy air which is very injurious, while it often gives the comic ones a ponderousness which is altogether singular, and but imperfectly accordant with the nature of comic dialogue. The arrows of Shakspeare's wit are not the lightly feathered shafts which Fletcher discharges, and as little are they the iron-headed bolts which fill the quiver of Jonson; but they are weapons forged from materials unknown to the others, and in an armoury to which they had no access; their execution is resistless when they reach their aim, but they are covered with a golden massiveness of decoration which sometimes impedes the swiftness of their flight. But whether the effect of these peculiarities of Shakspeare be good or evil, their use in helping an identification of his manner is very great. Nothing can be more directly opposite to them than the slow elegance and want of pointedness which we find in Fletcher, who is not free from conceits, but does not express them with Shakspeare's hard quaintness, while he is comparatively quite guiltless of plays on words. The following instances are only a few among many in the present drama, which seem to be perfectly in Shakspeare's manner, and to most of which Fletcher's works could certainly furnish no parallel, either in subject or in expression.

Oh, my petition was
Set down in ice, which, by hot grief uncandied,
Melts into tears; so sorrow wanting form
Is pressed with deeper matter.

Act I. Scene 1.

Theseus speaks thus of the Kinsmen lying before him in the field of battle desperately wounded:—

Rather than have them
Freed of this plight, and in their morning state,
Sound and at liberty, I would them dead:
But forty thousand fold we had rather have them
Prisoners to us than Death. Bear them speedily
From *our kind air, to them unkind,* and minister
What man to man may do.

Act I. Scene 4.

A lady hunting is addressed in this strain;

Oh jewel
O' the wood, O' the world!

Act III. Scene 1.

In the same scene one knight says to another,—

This question sick between us,
By bleeding must be cured.

And the one, left in the wood, says to the other, who goes to the presence of the lady whom both love—

> You talk of feeding me to breed me strength;
> You are going now to look upon a sun,
> That strengthens what *it* looks on.
>
> *Act III. Scene* 1.

The two knights, about to meet in battle, address each other in these words:—

> *Pal.* Think you but thus;
> That there were aught in me which strove to shew
> Mine enemy in this business, were't one eye
> Against another, arm opposed by arm,
> I would destroy the offender; coz, I would,
> Though parcel of myself: then from this gather
> How I should tender you!
> *Arc.* I am in labor
> To push your name, your ancient love, our kindred,
> Out of my memory, and i' the self-same place
> To seat something I would confound.
>
> *Act V. Scene* 1.

And afterwards their lady-love, listening to the noise of the fight, speaks thus:—

> Each stroke laments
> The place whereon it falls, and sounds more like
> A bell than blade.
>
> *Act V. Scene* 5.

Shakspeare's fondness for thought, the tendency of that train of thought to run into the abstract, and his burning imagination, have united in producing another quality which strongly marks his style, and is more pleasing than those last noticed. He abounds in Personification, and delights particularly in personifications of mental powers, passions, and relations. This metaphysico-poetical mood of musing tinges his miscellaneous poems deeply, especially the Venus and Adonis, which is almost lyrical throughout; and even in his dramas the style is often like one of Collins's exquisite odes. This quality is common to him with the narrative poets of his age, from whom he received it; but it is adopted to no material extent by any of his dramatic contemporaries, and by Fletcher less than any. The other dramatists, indeed, are full of metaphysical expressions, of the names of affections and faculties of the soul; but they do not go on as Shakspeare's kindling fancy impelled him to do, to look on them as independent and energetic existences. This figure is one of the most common means by which he elevates himself into the tragic and poetic sphere, the compromise between his reason and his imagination, the felicitous mode by which he reconciles his fondness for abstract thought with his allegiance to the genius of poetry. The Two Noble Kinsmen is rich in personifications both of mental qualities and others, which have all Shakspeare's tokens about them, and vary infinitely, from the uncompleted hint to the perfected portrait.

Oh Grief and Time,
Fearful consumers, you will all devour!
Act I. Scene 1.

Peace might purge
For her repletion, and retain anew
Her charitable heart, now hard, and harsher
Than Strife or War could be. *Act I. Scene* 2.

A most unbounded tyrant, whose success
Makes heaven unfeared, and villainy assured
Beyond its power there's nothing,—almost puts
Faith in a fever, and deifies alone
Voluble Chance. *Act I. Scene* 2.

This funeral path brings to your household graves;
Joy seize on you again—Peace sleep with him!
Act I. Scene 5.

Content and Anger
In me have but one face.
Act III. Scene 1.

Force and great Feat
Must put my garland on, where she will stick
The queen of flowers.
Act V. Scene 1.

Thou (*Love*) mayst force the king
To be his subject's vassal, and *induce*
Stale Gravity to dance;—the polled bachelor,
Whose youth, (like wanton boys through bonfires,)

Has skipt thy flame, at seventy thou canst catch,
And make him, to the scorn of his hoarse throat,
Abuse young lays of love.

Act V. Scene 2.

Mercy and manly Courage
Are bed-fellows in his visage.

Act V. Scene 5.

Our Reasons are not prophets,
When oft our Fancies are.

Act V. Scene 5.

The hints which you have now perused are not, I repeat, offered to you as by any means exhausting the elements of Shakspeare's manner of writing. They are meant only to bring to your memory such of his qualities of style as chiefly distinguish him from Fletcher, and are most prominently present in the play we are examining. When we shall see those qualities instanced singly, they will afford a proof of Shakspeare's authorship: but that proof will receive an incalculable accession of strength when, as will more frequently happen, we shall have several of them displayed at once in the same passages. Your recollection of them will serve us as the lines of a map would in a journey on foot through a wild forest country: the beauty of the landscape will tempt us not seldom to diverge and lose sight of our path, and we shall need their guidance for enabling us to regain it.

The story of Palamon and Arcite is a celebrated one, and, besides its appearance here, has been taken up by other two of our greatest English poets. Chaucer borrowed the tale from the *Teseide* of Boccaccio: it then received a dramatic form in this play; and from Chaucer's antique sketch it was afterwards decorated with the trappings of heroic rhyme by one who fell on evil days, the lofty and unfortunate Dryden. It treats of a period of ancient and almost fabulous history, which originally belonged to the classical writers, but had become familiar in the chivalrous poetry of the middle ages; and, retaining the old historical characters, it intersperses with them new ones wholly imaginary, and, both in the Knighte's Tale and in the play, preserves the rich and anomalous magnificence of the Gothic costume. The character round which the others are grouped, one which Shakspeare has introduced in another of his works, is the heroic Theseus, whom the romances and chronicles dignify with the modern title of Duke of Athens; and in this story he is connected with the tragical war of the Seven against Thebes, one of the grandest subjects of the ancient Grecian poetry.

The whole of the First Act may be safely pronounced to be Shakspeare's. The play opens with the bridal procession of Theseus and the fair Amazon Hippolita, whose young sister EMILIA is the lady of the tale. While the marriage-song is singing the train are met by three queens in mourning attire, who fall down at the feet of Theseus, Hippolita, and Emilia. They are the widows of three of the princes slain in battle before Thebes, and the conqueror Creon has refused the remains of the dead soldiers the last honour of a grave. The prayer of the unfortunate ladies to Theseus is, that he would raise his powerful arm to force from the tyrant the unburied corpses, that the ghosts of the dead may be appeased by the performance of fitting rites of sepulture. The duty which knighthood imposed on the Prince of Athens is combated by his unwillingness to quit his bridal happiness; but generosity and self-denial at length obtain the victory, and he marches with banners displayed to attack the Thebans.

This scene bears decided marks of Shakspeare.—The lyrical pieces scattered through his plays are, whether successful or not, endowed with a stateliness of rhythm, an originality and clearness of imagery, and a nervous quaintness and pomp of language, which can scarcely be mistaken. The Bridal Song which ushers in this play, has several of the marks of distinction, and is very unlike the more formal and polished rhymes of Fletcher.

* * * * *

Primrose, first-born child of Ver,
Merry springtime's harbinger,
With her bells dim;
Oxlips in their cradles growing,
Marigolds on death-beds blowing,
Lark-heels trim:
All, dear Nature's children sweet,
Lie 'fore bride and bridegroom's feet,

> *Blessing their sense:*
> Not an *angel of the air,*
> Bird melodious or bird fair,
> Be absent hence!
> * * * * *

But the dialogue which follows is strikingly characteristic. It has sometimes Shakspeare's identical images and words: it has his quaint force and sententious brevity, crowding thoughts and fancies into the narrowest space, and submitting to obscurity in preference to feeble dilation: it has sentiments enunciated with reference to subordinate relations, which other writers would have expressed with less grasp of thought: it has even Shakspeare's alliteration, and one or two of his singularities in conceit: it has clearness in the images taken separately, and confusion from the prodigality with which one is poured out after another, in the heat and hurry of imagination: it has both fulness of illustration and a variety which is drawn from the most distant sources; and it has, thrown over all, that air of originality and that character of poetry, the principle of which is often hid when their presence and effect are most quickly and instinctively perceptible.

> 1 *Queen. (To Theseus.)* For pity's sake and true gentility's,
> Hear and respect me!
> 2 *Queen. (To Hippolita.)* For your mother's sake,
> And as you wish your womb may thrive with fair ones,
> Hear and respect me!
> 3 *Queen (To Emilia.)* Now for the love of him whom Jove hath marked
> The honour of your bed, and for the sake
> Of clear virginity, be advocate
> For us and our distresses! This good deed
> Shall rase you out of the Book of Trespasses
> All you are set down there.

These latter lines are of a character which is perfectly and singularly Shakspeare's. The shade of gravity which so usually darkens his poetry, is often heightened to the most solemn seriousness. The religious thought presented here is most alien from Fletcher's turn of thought.—The ensuing speech offers much of Shakspeare. His energy, sometimes confined within due limits, often betrays him into harshness ; and his liking for familiarity of imagery and expression sometimes makes him careless though both should be coarse, a fault which we find here, and of which Fletcher is not guilty. Here also are more than one of those bold coinages of words, forced on a mind for whose force of conception common terms were too weak.

> 1 *Queen.* We are three queens, whose sovrans fell before
> The wrath of cruel Creon; who endured
> The beaks of ravens, talons of the kites,
> And pecks of crows, in the foul fields of Thebes.
> He will not suffer us to burn their bones,
> To *urn* their ashes, nor to take the offence
> Of mortal loathsomeness from the blest eye
> Of holy Phœbus, but infects the air
> With stench of our slain lords. Oh, pity, Duke!
> Thou purger* of the earth! draw thy feared sword,
> That does good turns i' the world: give us the bones
> Of our dead kings, that we may *chapel* them!
> And of thy boundless goodness take some note
> That for our crowned heads we have no roof
> Save this, which is the lion's and the bear's,
> And vault to every thing.

We now begin to trace more and more that reflective tendency which is so deeply imprinted on Shakspeare's writings.

> *Theseus.* * * * * *
> King Capaneus† was your lord: the day
> That he should marry you, at such a season
> As it is now with me, I met your groom
> By Mars's altar. You were that time fair;
> Not Juno's mantle fairer than your tresses,
> Nor in more bounty spread: your wheaten wreath
> Was then nor threshed nor blasted: Fortune at you
> Dimpled her cheek with smiles: Hercules our kinsman
> (Then weaker than your eyes) laid by his club,—
> He tumbled down upon his Nemean hide,

* Perhaps it is worth while to direct attention to this form of speech. Verbal names expressing the agent occur, it is true, in Fletcher and others, but they are in an especial manner frequent with Shakspeare, who invents them to preserve his brevity, and always applies them with great force and quaintness.

† Probably Fletcher would not have committed this false quantity.

And swore his sinews thawed. Oh, Grief and Time,
Fearful consumers, you will all devour!

1. *Queen.* Oh, I hope some god,
Some god hath put his mercy in your manhood,
Whereto he'll infuse power, and press you forth
Our undertaker!

Theseus. Oh, no knees; none, widow!
Unto the helmeted Bellona use them,
And pray for me your soldier.—Troubled I am. *(Turns away.)*

2 *Queen.* Honoured Hippolita, * * *
* * * * dear *glass of ladies!*
Bid him that we whom flaming war hath scorched
Under the shadow of his sword may cool us.
Require him he advance it o'er our heads;
Speak it in a woman's key, like such a woman
As any of us three: weep ere you fail;
Lend us a knee;—
But touch the ground for us no longer time
Than a dove's motion when the head's plucked off:
Tell him, if he i' the blood-sized field lay swollen,
Shewing the sun his teeth, grinning at the moon,
What you would do!

* * *

Emilia. Pray stand up;
Your grief is written on your cheek.

3 *Queen.* Oh, woe!
You cannot read it there: there (*in her eyes*) through my tears,
Like wrinkled pebbles in a glassy stream,
You may behold it. Lady, lady, alack!
He that will all the treasure know o' the earth
Must know the centre too: he that will fish
For my least minnow, let him lead his line
To catch one at my heart. Oh, pardon me!
Extremity, that sharpens sundry wits,
Makes me a fool.

Emilia. Pray you say nothing; pray you!
Who cannot feel nor see the rain, being in't,
Knows neither wet nor dry. If that you were
The ground-piece of some painter, I would buy you,
To instruct me 'gainst a capital grief indeed;
(Such heart-pierced demonstration;) but, alas!
Being a natural sister of our sex,
Your sorrow beats so ardently upon me,
That it shall make a counter-reflect against
My brother's heart, and warm it to some pity,
Though it were made of stone: Pray have good comfort!

* * *

1 *Queen.* (*To Theseus.*) * * Remember that your fame
Knolls in the ear o' the world: what you do quickly
Is not done rashly; your first thought is more
Than others' laboured meditance; your premeditating
More than their actions: but, (oh, Jove!) your actions,
Soon as they move, *as ospreys do the fish*,
Subdue before they touch. Think, dear duke, think
What beds our slain kings have.
2 *Queen.* What griefs our beds,
That our slain kings have none.

Theseus is moved by their prayers, but, loth to leave the side of his newly-wedded spouse, contents himself with directing his chief captain to lead the Athenian army against the tyrant. The queens redouble their entreaties for his personal aid.

2 *Queen.* We come unseasonably; but when could Grief
Cull out, as *unpanged Judgment* can, fitt'st time
For best solicitation!
Theseus. Why, good ladies,
This is a service whereto I am going,
Greater than any war: it more imports me
Than all the actions that I have foregone,
Or futurely can cope.
1 *Queen.* The more proclaiming
Our suit shall be neglected. When her arms,
Able to lock Jove from a synod, shall
By warranting moonlight *corslet* thee,—oh, when
Her twinning cherries shall their sweetness fall
Upon thy tasteful lips,—what wilt thou think
Of rotten kings or blubbered queens? what care
For what thou feel'st not, what thou feel'st being able
To make Mars spurn his drum?—Oh, if thou couch
But one night with her, every hour in't will
Take hostage of thee for a hundred, and
Thou shalt remember nothing more than what
That banquet bids thee to.
* * *
Theseus. Pray stand up:
I am entreating of myself to do
That which you kneel to have me. Perithous?
Lead on the bride! Get you and pray the gods
For success and return; omit not any thing
In the pretended celebration. Queens!
Follow your soldier. * *

* * (*To Hippolita.*) Since that our theme is haste,
I stamp this kiss upon thy currant lip:
Sweet, keep it as my token! * *

1 *Queen.* Thus dost thou still make good the tongue o' the world.
2 *Queen.* And earn'st a deity equal with Mars.
3 *Queen.* If not above him; for
Thou, being but mortal, mak'st affections bend
To godlike honours: *they themselves, some say,*
Groan under such a mastery.
Theseus. As we are men,
Thus should we do: being sensually subdued,
We lose our human title. Good cheer, ladies!
Now turn we towards your comforts. (*Exeunt.*)

The second scene introduces the heroes of the piece, Palamon and Arcite. They are two youths of the blood-royal of Thebes, who follow the banners of their sovereign with a sense that obedience is their duty, but under a sorrowful conviction that his cause is unjust, and their country rotten at the core. The scene is a dialogue between them, occupied in lamentations and repinings over the dissolute manners of their native Thebes. Its broken versification points out Shakspeare: the quaintness of some conceits is his; and several of the phrases and images have much of his pointedness, brevity, or obscurity. The scene, though not lofty in tone, does not want interest, and contains some extremely original illustrations. But quotations will be multiplied abundantly before we have done; and their number must not be increased by the admission of any which are not either unusually good or very distinctly characteristic of their author. Some lines of the scene have been already given.

The third scene has the farewell commendations of the young Emilia and her sister to Perithous, when he sets out to join Theseus, then before the Theban walls, and a subsequent conversation of the two ladies. Much of this scene has Shakspeare's stamp deeply cut upon it: it is probably all his. It is identified, not only by several others of the qualities marking the first scene, but more particularly by the wealth of its allusion, and by a closeness, directness, and pertinency of reply which Fletcher's most spirited dialogues do not reach. It presents more than one exceedingly beautiful climax; a figure which repeatedly occurs in the play, and is always used with peculiar energy.

SCENE—*Before the Gates of Athens.—Enter Perithous, Hippolita, and Emilia.*

Perithous. No further.
Hippolita. Sir, farewell. Repeat my wishes
To our great lord, of whose success I dare not
Make any timorous question; yet I wish him
Excess and overflow of power, an't might be,
To dure ill-dealing Fortune. Speed to him!
Store never hurts good governors.
Perithous. Though I know
His ocean needs not my poor drops, yet they
Must yield their tribute there. (*To Emilia.*) My precious maid,
Those best affections that the heavens infuse
In their *best-tempered pieces,* keep *enthroned*
In your dear heart!
Emilia. Thanks, sir! Remember me
To our all-royal brother, for whose speed
The great Bellona I'll solicit; and,
Since in our terrene state petitions are not
Without gifts understood, I'll offer to her
What I shall be advised she likes. Our hearts
Are in his army, in his tent.
Hippolita. In's bosom!
We have been soldiers, and we cannot weep
When our friends don their helms or put to sea,
Or tell of babes broached on the lance, or women
That have sod their infants in (and after eat them)
The brine they wept at killing them; then if
You stay to see of us such spinsters, we
Should hold you here for ever.
* * *
Emilia. How his longing
Follows his friend! * *
* * Have you observed him
Since our great lord departed?
Hippolita. With much labour,
And I did love him for't.* * *

* The remainder of this speech, an extremely fine one, has been quoted incidentally in page 18. Its richness of fancy is wonderful and most characteristic.

The description of female friendship which follows is familiar to all lovers of poetry. It is disfigured by one or two strained conceits, and some obscurities arising partly from errors in the text: but the beauty of the sketch in many parts is extreme, and its character distinctly that of Shakspeare, vigorous and even quaint, thoughtful and sometimes almost metaphysical, instinct with animation, and pregnant with fancy; offering, in short, little resemblance to the manner of any poet but Shakspeare, and the most unequivocal opposition to Fletcher's.

Emilia. Doubtless
There is a best, and reason has no manners
To say, it is not you. I was acquainted
Once with a time when I enjoyed a playfellow——
You were at wars when she the grave enriched,
(Who made too proud the bed,) took leave o' the moon,
Which then looked pale at parting, when our count
Was each eleven.
Hippolita. 'Twas Flavina.
Emilia. Yes.
You talk of Perithous' and Theseus' love:
Theirs has more ground, is more maturely seasoned,
More buckled with strong judgment; and their needs
The one of the other may be said to water
Their intertangled roots of love.—But I
And she I sigh and spoke of, were things innocent,—
Loved for we did, and,—like the elements,
That know not what nor why, yet do effect
Rare issues by their operance,—our souls
Did so to one another. What she liked,
Was then of me approved; what not, condemned.
No more arraignment. The flower that I would pluck,
And put between my breasts, (then but beginning
To swell about the blossom,) she would long
Till she had such another, and commit it
To the like innocent cradle, where, phœnix-like,
They died in perfume; on my head no toy
But was her pattern; her affections, (pretty,
Though happily her careless wear,) I followed
For my most serious decking.—Had mine ear
Stolen some new air, or at adventure hummed
From musical coinage,—why, it was a note
Whereon her spirits would sojourn, rather dwell on,
And sing it in her slumbers.—This rehearsal

(Which, every innocent wots well, comes in
Like old importment's bastard) has this end,
That the true love 'tween maid and maid may be
More than in sex dividual. * *

The fourth scene is laid in a battle-field near Thebes, and Theseus enters victorious. The three queens fall down with thanks before him ; and a herald announces the capture of the Two Noble Kinsmen, wounded and senseless, and scarcely retaining the semblance of life. The phraseology of this short scene is like Shakspeare's, being brief and energetic, and in one or two instances passing into quibbles.

The last scene of this act is of a lyrical cast, and comprised in a few lamentations spoken by the widowed queens over the corpses of their dead lords. It ends with this couplet :

The world's a city full of straying streets,
And death's the market-place, where each one meets.

In the Second Act no part seems to have been taken by Shakspeare. It commences with one of those scenes which are introduced into the play in departure from the narrative of Chaucer, forming an underplot which is clearly the work of a different artist from many of the leading parts of the drama. The Noble Kinsmen, cured of their wounds, have been committed to strait and perpetual prison in Athens, and the first part of this scene is a prose dialogue between their jailor and a suitor of his daughter. The maiden's admiration of the prisoners is then exhibited. You will see afterwards, that there are several circumstances besides the essential dullness of this prose part, which fully absolve Shakspeare from the charge of having written it.

The versified portion of this scene, which follows the prose dialogue among the inferior characters, presents the incident on which the interest of the story hinges, the commencement of the fatal and chimerical passion, which, inspiring both the knights towards the young Emilia, severs the bonds of friendship which had so long held them together. The noble prisoners are discovered in their turret-chamber, looking out on the palace-garden, which the lady afterwards enters. They speak in a highly animated strain of that world from which they are secluded, and find themes of consolation for the hard lot which had overtaken them. The dialogue is in many respects admirable. It possesses much eloquence of description, and the character of the language is smooth and flowing; the versification is good and accurate, frequent in double endings, and usually finishing the sense with the line; and one or two allusions occur, which, being favourites of Fletcher's, may be in themselves a strong presumption of his authorship; the images too have in some instances a want of distinctness in application or a vagueness of outline, which could be easily paralleled from Fletcher's acknowledged writings. The style is fuller of allusions than his usually is, but the images are more correct and better kept from confusion than Shakspeare's; some of them indeed are exquisite, but rather in the romantic and exclusively poetical tone of Fletcher, than in the natural and universal mode of feeling which animates Shakspeare. The dialogue too proceeds less energetically than Shakspeare's, falling occasionally into a style of long-drawn disquisition which Fletcher often substitutes for the quick and dramatic conversations of the great poet. On the whole, however, this scene, if it be Fletcher's, (of which I have no doubt,) is among the very finest he ever wrote; and there are many passages in which, while he preserves his own distinctive marks, he has gathered no small portion of the flame and inspiration of his immortal friend and assistant. In the following speeches there are images and phrases, which are either identically Fletcher's, or closely resemble his, and the whole cast both of versification and idiom is strictly his.

Palamon. Oh, cousin Arcite!
Where is Thebes now? where is our noble country?
Where are our friends and kindreds? Never more
Must we behold those comforts; never see
The hardy youths strive in the games of honour,
Hung with the painted favours of their ladies,
Like tall ships under sail; then start among them,
And as an east wind leave them all behind us
Like lazy clouds, while Palamon and Arcite,
Even in the wagging of a wanton leg,
Outstript the people's praises, won the garlands,

Ere they have time to wish them ours. Oh, never
Shall we two exercise, like twins of honour,
Our arms again, and feel our fiery horses
Like proud seas under us! our good swords now,
(Better the red-eyed god of war ne'er wore,)
Ravished our sides, like age must run to rust,
And deck the temples of the gods that hate us:
These hands shall never draw them out like lightning
To blast whole armies more.

Arcite. * * *
The sweet embraces of a loving wife,
Loaden with kisses, armed with thousand cupids,
Shall never clasp our necks: no issue know us;
No figures of ourselves shall we e'er see,
To glad our age, and like young eagles teach them
Boldly to gaze against bright arms, and say,
"Remember what your fathers were, and conquer."
—The fair-eyed maids shall weep our banishments,
And in their songs curse ever-blinded Fortune,
Till she for shame see what a wrong she has done
To Youth and Nature.—This is all our world:
We shall know nothing here but one another,—
Hear nothing but the clock that tells our woes;
The vine shall grow, but we shall never see it:
Summer shall come, and with her all delights,
But dead-cold winter must inhabit here still!

Palamon. 'Tis too true, Arcite! To our Theban hounds,
That shook the aged forest with their echoes,
No more now must we halloo; no more shake
Our pointed javelins, whilst the angry swine
Flies like a Parthian* quiver from our rages,
Struck with our well-steeled darts. * *

In this scene there is one train of metaphors which is perhaps as characteristic of Fletcher as any thing that could be produced. It is marked by a slowness of association which he often shews. Several allusions are successively introduced; but by each as it appears we are prepared for and can anticipate the next: we see the connexion of ideas in the poet's mind through which the one has sprung out of the other, and that all are but branches, of which one original thought is the root. All this is the work of

* This allusion is repeatedly found in Fletcher. Here the expression of it is defective in precision.

a less fertile fancy and a more tardy understanding than Shakspeare's: he would have leaped over many of the intervening steps, and, reaching at once the most remote particular of the series, would have immediately turned away to weave some new chain of thought.

> *Arcite.* * * What worthy blessing
> Can be, but our imaginations
> May make it ours? and here, being thus together,
> We are an endless mine to one another:
> We are one another's wife, ever begetting
> New births of love; we are fathers, friends, acquaintance;
> We are, in one another, families;
> I am your heir and you are mine; this place
> Is our inheritance; no hard oppressor
> Dare take this from us. * *

But the contentment of the prison is to be interrupted. The fair Emilia appears beneath, walking in the garden "full of branches green," skirting the wall of the tower in which the princes are confined. She converses with her attendant, and Palamon from the dungeon-grating beholds her as she gathers the flowers of spring. He ceases to reply to Arcite, and stands absorbed in silent extacy.

> *Arcite.* Cousin! How do you, sir? Why, Palamon!
> *Palamon.* Never till now I was in prison, Arcite.
> *Arcite.* Why, what's the matter, man?
> *Palamon.* Behold and wonder:
> By Heaven, she is a goddess!
> *Arcite.* Ha!
> *Palamon.* Do reverence;
> She is a goddess, Arcite!

The beauty of the maiden impresses Arcite no less violently than it previously had his kinsman; and he challenges with great heat a right to love her. An animated and acrimonious dialogue ensues, in which Palamon reproachfully pleads his prior admiration of the lady, and insists on his cousin's obligation to become his abettor instead of his rival. It is spirited even to excess; and probably Shakspeare would have tempered or abstained from treating so sudden and perhaps unnatural an access of anger and jealousy, and so utter an abandonment to its vehemence, as that under which the fiery Palamon is here represented as labouring.

Palamon. If thou lovest her,
Or entertain'st a hope to blast my wishes,
Thou art a traitor, Arcite, and a fellow
False as thy title to her. Friendship, blood,
And all the ties between us, I disclaim,
If thou once think upon her!
Arcite. Yes, I love her!
And, if the lives of all my name lay on it,
I must do so. I love her with my soul;
If that will lose thee, Palamon, farewell!
I say again I love, and, loving her
I am as worthy and as free a lover,
And have as just a title to her beauty,
As any Palamon, or any living
That is a man's son!
Palamon. Have I called thee friend!
* * *
Palamon. Put but thy head out of this window more,
And, as I have a soul, I'll nail thy life to't!
Arcite. Thou darest not, fool: thou canst not: thou art feeble:
Put my head out? I'll throw my body out,
And leap the garden, when I see her next,
And pitch between her arms to anger thee.

In transferring his story from Chaucer, the poet has here been guilty of an oversight. The old poet fixes a character of positive guilt on Arcite's prosecution of his passion, by relating a previous agreement between the two cousins, by which either, engaging in any adventure whether of love or war, had an express right to the co-operation of the other. Hence Arcite's interference with his cousin's claim becomes with Chaucer a direct infringement of a knightly compact; while in the drama no deeper blame attaches to it than as a violation of the more fragile rules imposed by the generous spirit of friendship.

In the midst of the angry conference Arcite is called to the Duke to receive his freedom; and Palamon is placed in stricter confinement, and removed from the quarter of the tower overlooking the garden.

In the second scene of this act, Arcite, wandering in the

neighbourhood of Athens, soliloquizes on the decree which had banished him from the Athenian territory; and, falling in with a band of country people on their way to games in the city, conceives the notion of joining in the celebration under some poor disguise, in the hope of finding means to remain within sight of his fancifully beloved mistress. Neither this scene, nor the following, in which the jailor's daughter meditates on the perfections of Palamon, and intimates an intention of assisting him to escape, have any thing in them worthy of particular notice.

In the fourth scene, Arcite, victorious in the athletic games, is crowned by the Duke, and preferred to the service of Emilia.

In the last scene of the second act, the jailor's daughter announces that she has effected Palamon's deliverance from prison, and that he lies hidden in a wood near the city, the scenery of which is prettily described.

Nothing in the Third Act can with confidence be attributed to Shakspeare, except the first scene. This opening scene is laid in the wood where Palamon has his hiding-place. Arcite enters, and a monologue, describing his situation and feelings, is, as in Chaucer, overheard by Palamon, who starts out of the bush in which he had crouched, and shakes his fettered hands at his false kinsman. A dialogue of mutual reproach ensues, and Arcite departs with a promise to return, bringing food for the outcast, and armour to fit him for maintaining, like a knight, his right to the lady's love. The commencing speech of Arcite has much of Shakspeare's clearness of imagery, and of the familiarity of dress which he often loves to bestow upon allusion; it has also great nerve of expression and calmness of tone, with at least one play on words which is quite in his manner, and one (perhaps more) of his identical phrases. The text seems faulty in one part.

Arcite. The Duke has lost Hippolita: each took
A several laund. This is a solemn rite
They owe bloomed May, and the Athenians pay it
To the heart of ceremony. Oh, queen Emilia!
Fresher than May, sweeter
Than her *gold buttons* on the boughs, or all

The enamelled knacks o' the mead or garden! Yea,
We challenge too the bank of any nymph,
That makes the stream seem flowers!—Thou,—oh jewel
O' the wood, o' the world,—hast likewise blest a place
With thy sole presence. In thy rumination
That I, poor man, might eftsoons come between,
And chop on some cold thought!—Thrice blessed chance,
To drop on such a mistress! Expectation
Most guiltless of it. Tell me, oh lady Fortune,
(Next after Emily my sovran,) how far
I may be proud. She takes strong note of me,
Hath made me near her, and this beauteous morn,
(The primest of all the year,) presents me with
A brace of horses; two such steeds might well
Be by a pair of kings backed, in a field
That their crowns' titles tried. Alas, alas!
Poor cousin Palamon, poor prisoner! * *
* * * * If
Thou knew'st my mistress breathed on me, and that
I *eared* her language, lived in her eye, oh coz,
What passion would enclose thee!

There is great spirit, also, in what follows. Some phrases, here again, are precisely Shakspeare's; and several parts of the dialogue have much of his pointed epigrammatic style. The massive accumulation of reproaches which Palamon hurls on Arcite is, in its energy, more like him than his assistant; and the opposition of character between Palamon and his calmer kinsman, is well kept up; but the dialogue cannot be accounted one of the best in the play.

Palamon. * * Oh, thou most perfidious
That ever gently looked! The void'st of honour
That e'er bore gentle token! Falsest cousin
That ever blood made kin! call'st thou her thine?
I'll prove it in my shackles, in these hands
Void of appointment, that thou liest, and art
A very thief in love, a chaffy lord,
Not worth the name of villain!—Had I a sword,
And these house-clogs away!
Arcite. *Dear cousin Palamon!*
Palamon. Cozener Arcite! give me language such
As thou hast shewed me feat.
Arcite. Not finding in

The circuit of my breast any gross stuff
To form me like your *blazon*, holds me to
This gentleness of answer. 'Tis your passion
That thus mistakes; the which, to you being enemy,
Cannot to me be kind. * *

In the second scene the only speaker is the jailor's daughter, who, having lost Palamon in the wood, begins to shew symptoms of unsettled reason. There is some pathos in several parts of her soliloquy, but little vigour in the expression, or novelty in the thoughts.

The third scene is an exchange of brief speeches between the two knights. Arcite brings provisions for his kinsman, and the means of removing his fetters, and departs to fetch the armour. In most respects the scene is not very characteristic of either writer, but leans towards Fletcher; and one argument for him might be drawn from an interchange of sarcasms between the kinsmen, in which they retort on each other former amorous adventures: such a dialogue is quite like Fletcher's men of gaiety; and needless degradation of his principal characters is a fault of which Shakspeare is not guilty. You may be able, hereafter, to see more distinctly the force of this reason. The scene contains one strikingly animated burst of jealous suspicion and impatience.

Arcite. Pray you sit down then; and let me entreat you,
By all the honesty and honour in you,
No mention of this woman; 'twill disturb us;
We shall have time enough.
Palamon. Well, sir, I'll pledge you.
* * * *
Arcite. Heigh-ho!
Palamon. For Emily, upon my life!—Fool,
Away with this strained mirth!—I say again,
That sigh was breathed for Emily. Base cousin,
Darest thou break first?
Arcite. You are wide.
Palamon. By heaven and earth,
There's nothing in thee honest! * *

In the next two scenes, placed in the forest, the jailor's daughter has reached the height of frenzy. She meets the countrymen who had encountered Arcite, and who are now headed by the learned and high-fantastical schoolmaster Gerrold, a personage who has the pedantry of Shakspeare's Holofernes, without one solitary spark of his humour. They are preparing a dance for the presence of the duke, and the maniac is adopted into their number, to fill up a vacancy. The duke and his train appear,—the pedagogue prologuizes,—the clowns dance,—and their self-satisfied Coryphaeus apologizes and epiloguizes. Some of Fletcher's very phrases and forms of expression have been traced in these two scenes.

We have then, in the sixth and last scene of this act, the interrupted combat of the two princes. The scene is a spirited and excellent one; but its tone is Fletcher's, not Shakspeare's. The raillery and retort of the dialogue is more lightly playful than his, and less antithetical and sententious; and though there are fine images, they are not seized with the grasp which Shakspeare would have given, sometimes harsh, but always at least decided. Some of the illustrations have been quoted, (page 16.) The knightly courtesy with which the princes arm each other is well supported; and their dignity of greeting before they cross their swords, is fine, exceedingly fine. Nothing can be more beautifully conceived than the change which comes over the temper of the generous Palamon, when he stands on the verge of mortal battle with his enemy. His usual heat and impatience give place to the most becoming calmness. The versification is very sweet, and the romantic air of the phraseology is very much Fletcher's, especially towards the end of the following quotation.

Palamon. My cause and honour guard me!
(They bow several ways, then advance and stand.)
Arcite. And me my love! Is there aught else to say?
Palamon. This only, and no more: Thou art mine aunt's son,
And that blood we desire to shed is mutual,
In me thine, and in thee mine. My sword
Is in my hand, and, if thou killest me,
The gods and I forgive thee! If there be
A place prepared for those that sleep in honour,
I wish his weary soul that falls may win it!
Fight bravely, cousin; give me thy noble hand!

Arcite. Here, Palamon; this hand shall never more
Come near thee with such friendship.
Palamon. I commend thee.
Arcite. If I fall, curse me, and say I was a coward;
For none but such dare die in these just trials.
Once more farewell, my cousin.
Palamon. Farewell, Arcite.
(They fight.)

The combat is interrupted by the approach of the Duke and his court; and Palamon, refusing to give back or conceal himself, appears before Theseus, and declares his own name and situation, and the presumptuous secret of Arcite. The scene is good, but in the flowing style of Fletcher, not the more manly one of Shakspeare. The sentence of death which the duke, in the first moments of his anger, pronounces on the two princes, is recalled on the petition of Hippolita and her sister, on condition that the rivals shall meantime depart, and return within a month, each accompanied by three knights, to determine in combat the possession of Emilia; and death by the block is denounced against the knights who shall be vanquished. Some of these circumstances are slight deviations from Chaucer; and the laying down of the severe penalty is well imagined, as an addition to the tragic interest, giving occasion to a very impressive scene in the last act.

The Fourth Act may safely be pronounced wholly Fletcher's. All of it, except one scene, is taken up by the episodical adventures of the jailor's daughter; and while much of it is poetical, it wants the force and originality, and, indeed, all the prominent features of Shakspeare's manner, either of thought, illustration, or expression. There are conversations in which are described, pleasingly enough, the madness of the unfortunate girl, and the finding of her in a sylvan spot, by her former wooer; but when the maniac herself appears, the tone and subjects of the dialogue become more objectionable.

In the second scene of this act, the only one which bears reference to the main business of the piece, Emilia first muses over the pictures of her two suitors, and then hears from a messenger, in presence of Theseus and his attendants, a description, (taken in its elements from the Knighte's Tale,) of the warriors who were preparing for the field along with the champion lovers. In the soliloquy of the lady, while the poetical spirit is well preserved, the alternations of feeling are given with an abruptness and a want of insight into the nicer shades of association, which resemble the extravagant stage effects of the King and No King, infinitely more than the delicate yet piercing glance with which Shakspeare looks into the human breast in the Othello; the language, too, is smoother and less powerful than Shakspeare's, and one or two classical allusions are a little too correct and studied for him. One image occurs, not the clearest or most chastened, in which Fletcher closely repeats himself.

What a brow,
Of what a spacious majesty, he carries!
Arched like the great-eyed Juno's, but far sweeter,—
Smoother than Pelops' shoulder. Fame and Honour
Methinks, from hence as from a promontory
Pointed in Heaven, should clap their wings, and sing
To all the under-world the loves and fights
Of gods and such men near them.*

In the Fifth Act we again feel the presence of the Master of the Spell. Several passages in this portion are marked by as striking tokens of his art as any thing which we read in Macbeth or Coriolanus. The whole act, a very long one, may be boldly attributed to him, with the exception of one episodical scene.

The time has arrived for the combat. Three temples are exhibited, as in Chaucer, in which the rival Knights and the

* In Philaster, Act IV. last Scene.
Place me, some god, upon a Piramis,
Higher than hill of earth, and lend a voice
Loud as your thunder to me, that from thence
I may discourse to all the under world
The worth that dwells in him.

Shakspeare, too, was not the most likely person to have given the true meaning of the βοωπις ποτνια Ἥρη. I am not aware that either Hall or Chapman shewed him the way. Chapman in the First Book, (v. 551) has it; "She with the cowes fair eyes, Respected Juno."

Lady of their Vows respectively pay their adorations. One principal aim of their supplications is to learn the result of the coming contest; but the suspense is kept up by each of the knights receiving a favourable response, and Emilia a doubtful one. Three scenes are thus occupied, the second of which is in somewhat a lower key than the other two; but even in it there is much beauty; and in the first and third, the tense dignity and pointedness of the language, the gorgeousness and overflow of illustration, and the reach, the mingled familiarity and elevation of thought, are admirable, inimitable, and decisive. From these exquisite scenes there is a temptation to quote too largely.

In the first scene Theseus ushers the Kinsmen and their Knights into the Temple of Mars, and leaves them there. After a short and solemn greeting, the Kinsmen embrace for the last time, Palamon and his friends retire, and Arcite and his remain and offer up their devotions to the deity of the place. A fine seriousness of spirit breathes through the whole scene, and the language is alive with the most magnificent and delicate allusion. In Arcite's prayer the tone cannot be mistaken. The enumeration of the god's attributes is coloured by all that energetic depth of feeling with which Shakspeare in his historical dramas so often turns aside to meditate on the changes of human fortune and the horrors of human enmity.*

* * *

Theseus. You valiant and strong-hearted enemies,
You royal germane foes, that this day come
To blow the nearness out that flames between ye,—
Lay by your anger for an hour, and dove-like,
Before the holy altars of your Helpers
(The all-feared Gods) bow down your stubborn bodies!
Your ire is more than mortal: so your help be!

* * *

Arcite. * * Hoist we
Those sails that must these vessels port even where
The Heavenly Limiter pleases!

* * *

* This beautiful address has been spoken of already.

Knights, kinsmen, lovers, yea, my sacrifices!
True worshippers of Mars, whose spirit in you
Expels the seeds of fear, and the apprehension
Which still is father of it,—go with me
Before the god of our profession. There
Require of him the hearts of lions, and
The breath of tigers, yea the fierceness too,
Yea the speed also! to go on I mean,
Else wish we to be snails. You know my prize
Must be dragged out of blood: Force and great Feat
Must put my garland on, where she will stick
The queen of flowers; our intercession then
Must be to him that makes the camp *a cestron*
Brimmed with the blood of men: give me your aid,
And bend your spirits towards him!

(They fall prostrate before the statue.)

Thou mighty one! that with thy power hast turned
Green Neptune into purple,—whose approach
Comets prewarn,—*whose havock in vast field*
Unearthed skulls proclaim,—whose breath blows down
The teeming Ceres' foyson,—who dost pluck
With hand armipotent from forth blue clouds
The masoned turrets,—that both mak'st and break'st
The stony girths of cities;—me thy pupil,
Young'st follower of thy drum, instruct this day
With military skill, that to thy laud
I may advance my streamer, and by thee
Be styled the lord o' the day: Give me, great Mars,
Some token of thy pleasure!

(Here there is heard clanging of armour, with a short thunder, as the burst of a battle; whereupon they all rise and bow to the altar.)

Oh, great Corrector of enormous times!
Shaker of o'er-rank states! Thou grand Decider
Of dusty and old titles;—*that heal'st with blood*
The earth when it is sick, and curest the world
O' the pleurisy of people! I do take
Thy signs auspiciously, and in thy name
To my design march boldly. Let us go! *(Exeunt.)*

The passionate and sensitive Palamon has chosen the Queen Love as his Patroness, and it is in her Temple that, in the second scene, he puts up his prayers. This scene is not equal to the first or third, having the poetical features less prominently brought out, while the tone of thought is less highly pitched, and also less consistently sustained. But it is distinctly Shakspeare's. The rugged versification is his, and the force of language. One unpleasing sketch of the deformity of decrepid old age, which need not be quoted, is largely impressed with his air of truth, and some personifications already noticed are also in his manner.

Palamon. Our stars must glister with new fire, or be
To-day extinct: our argument is love!
* * *(They kneel.)*
Hail, sovereign Queen of Secrets! who hast power
To call the fiercest tyrant from his rage
To weep unto a girl!—that hast the might
Even with an eye-glance to choke Mars's drum,
And turn the alarm to whispers! * *
* * What god-like power
Hast thou not power upon? To Phœbus thou
Add'st flames hotter than his: the heavenly fires
Did scorch his mortal son, thou him: The Huntress
All moist and cold, some say, began to throw
Her bow away and sigh. Take to thy grace
Me thy vowed soldier,—who do bear thy yoke
As 'twere a wreath of roses, yet is heavier
Than lead itself, stings more than nettles:—
I have never been foul-mouthed against thy law;
* * I have been harsh
To large confessors, and have hotly asked them
If they had mothers: *I* had one,—a woman,
And women 'twere they wronged. * *
* * Brief,—I am
To those that prate and have done,—no companion;
To those that boast and have not,—a defier;
To those that would and cannot,—a rejoicer!
Yea, him I do not love, that tells close offices
The foulest way, nor names concealments in
The boldest language: Such a one I am,
And vow that *lover never yet made sigh*
Truer than I. * *

(Music is heard, and doves are seen to flutter: they fall upon their faces.)

* I give thee thanks
For this fair token! * *

Emilia's Prayer in the Sanctuary of the pure Diana, forming the third scene, is in some parts most nervous, and the opening is inexpressibly beautiful in language and rhythm. Several ideas and idioms are identically Shakspeare's.

Emilia. (Kneeling before the altar.) Oh, sacred, shadowy, cold, and constant Queen!
Abandoner of revels! mute, contemplative,
Sweet, solitary, white as chaste, and pure
As wind-fanned snow!—who to thy *female knights*
Allow'st no more blood than will make a blush,
Which is their order's robe!—I here, thy priest,
Am humbled 'fore thine altar. Oh, vouchsafe,
With that thy rare *green eye,* * which never yet
Beheld thing maculate, look on thy virgin!
And,—sacred silver Mistress!—lend thine ear,
(Which ne'er heard scurril term, into whose port
Ne'er entered wanton sound,) to my petition
Seasoned with holy fear!—This is my last
Of vestal office: I'm bride-habited,
But maiden-hearted. A husband I have appointed,
But do not know him; out of two I should
Chuse one, and pray for his success, but I
Am guiltless of election of mine eyes.
* * *

(A rose-tree ascends from under the altar, having one rose upon it.)

See what our general of ebbs and flows
Out from the bowels of her holy altar
With sacred act advances! But one rose?
If well inspired, this battle shall confound
Both these brave knights, and I a virgin flower
Must grow alone unplucked.

(Here is heard a sudden twang of instruments, and the rose falls from the tree.)

* Romeo and Juliet:—Midsummer Night's Dream:—also in Don Quixote, Parte II. capit. xi: "Los ojos de Dulcinea deben ser de *verdes esmeraldas.*"

> The flower is fallen, the tree descends!—oh, mistress,
> Thou here dischargest me: I shall be gathered,
> I think so; but I know not thine own will;
> Unclasp thy mystery!—I hope she's pleased;
> Her signs were gracious. *(Exeunt.)*

The fourth scene, in which the characters are the jailor's daughter, her father and lover, and a physician, is disgusting and imbecile in the extreme. It may be dismissed with a single quotation.

> *Doctor.* What stuff she utters.

The fifth scene is the Combat, the arrangement of which is unusual. Perhaps there is nothing in every respect resembling it in the circle of the English drama. Theseus and his court cross the stage as proceeding to the lists; Emilia pauses and refuses to be present; the rest depart, and she is left. She then, the prize of the struggle, the presiding influence of the day, alone occupies the stage: within, the trumpets are heard sounding the charge, and the cries of the spectators and tumult of the encounter reach her ears; one or two messengers recount to her the various changes of the field, till Arcite's victory ends the fight. The manner is admirable in which the caution, which rendered it advisable to avoid introducing the combat on the stage, is reconciled with the pomp of scenic effect and bustle. The details of the scene, with which alone we have here to do, make it clear that Shakspeare's hand was in it. The greater part, it is true, is not of the highest excellence; but the vacillations of Emilia's feelings are well and delicately given, some individual thoughts and words mark Shakspeare, there is a little of his obscure brevity, much of his thoughtfulness legitimately applied, and an instance or two of its abuse. The strong likeness to him will justify some quotations.

In the following lines Theseus is pleading with Emilia for her presence in the lists.

> *Theseus.* You must be there:
> This trial is as 'twere in the night, and you
> The'only star to shine.

Emilia. I am extinct.
There is but envy in that light, which shews
The one the other. Darkness, which ever was
The dam of Horror, who does stand accursed
Of many mortal millions, may even now,
By casting her black mantle over both
That neither could find other, get herself
Some part of a good name, and many a murder
Set off whereto she's guilty.*
* * *

One good description is put into the mouth of Emilia after she is left alone.

Emilia. Arcite is gently visaged; yet his eye
Is like an engine bent, or a sharp weapon
In a soft sheath: Mercy and manly Courage
Are bedfellows in his visage. Palamon
Has a most menacing aspect: his brow
Is graved, and seems to bury what it frowns on;
Yet sometimes 'tis not so, but alters to
The quality of his thoughts: long time his eye
Will dwell upon his object: melancholy
Becomes him nobly; so does Arcite's mirth:
But Palamon's sadness is a kind of mirth,
So mingled, as if mirth did make him sad,
And sadness merry: those darker humours that
Stick unbecomingly on others, on him
Live in fair dwelling.

After several alternations of fortune in the fight, she again speaks thus of the two:

* * Were they metamorphosed
Both into one—oh why? there were no woman
Worth so composed a man! their single share,
Their nobleness peculiar to them, gives
The prejudice of disparity, value's shortness,
To any lady breathing. * *
(*Cornets: a great shout, and cry,* Arcite, victory!)

* The thought here is frequent in Shakspeare's dramas: and the expression of it closely resembles some stanzas in the Lucrece, especially those beginning, "Oh, comfort-killing night!"

Servant. The cry is
Arcite and victory! Hark, Arcite, victory!
The combat's consummation is proclaimed
By the wind instruments.
Emilia. Half-sights saw
That Arcite was no babe: god's-lid! *his richness*
And costliness of spirit looked through him: it could
No more be hid in him than fire in flax,
Than humble banks can go to law with waters
That drift winds force to raging. I did think
Good Palamon would miscarry; yet I knew not
Why I did think so. *Our Reasons are not prophets*
When oft our Fancies are. They're coming off:
Alas, poor Palamon!

Theseus enters with his attendants, conducting Arcite, as conqueror, and presents him to Emilia as her husband. Arcite's situation is a painful one, and is well discriminated: he utters but a single grave sentence.

Theseus. (To Arcite and Emilia.) Give me your hands:
Receive you her, you him: be plighted with
A love that grows as you decay!
Arcite. Emily!
To buy you I have lost what's dearest to me,
Save what is bought; and yet I purchase cheaply,
As I do rate your value.

* * *

Theseus. (To Arcite.) Wear the garland
With joy that you have won. For the subdued,—
Give them our present justice, *since I know*
Their lives but pinch them. Let it here be done.
The sight's not for our seeing: go we hence
Right joyful, with some sorrow!—Arm your prize:
I know you will not lose her. Hippolita,
I see one eye of yours conceives a tear,
The which it will deliver.
Emilia. Is this winning?
Oh, all you heavenly powers! where is your mercy?
But that your wills have said it must be so,
And charge me live to comfort this unfriended,
This miserable prince, that cuts away
A life more worthy from him than all women,
I should and would die too.

Hippolita. Infinite pity,
That four such eyes should be so fixed on one,
That two must needs be blind for't. *(Exeunt.)*

The authorship of the last scene admits of no doubt. The manner is Shakspeare's, and some parts are little inferior to his very finest passages. Palamon has been vanquished, and he and his friends are to undergo execution of the sentence to which the laws of the combat subjected them. The depth of the interest is now fixed on these unfortunate knights, and a fine spirit of resigned melancholy inspires the scene in which they pass to their deaths.*

(Enter Palamon and his knights, pinioned; jailor, executioner, and guard.)

Palamon. There's many a man alive that hath outlived
The love of the people; yea, in the self-same state
Stands many a father with his child; some comfort
We have by so considering. We expire,—
And not without men's pity;—to live still,
Have their good wishes. We prevent
The loathsome misery of age, beguile
The gout and rheum, that in lag hours attend
For grey approachers. We come towards the gods
Young and unwarped, not halting under crimes
Many and stale; that sure shall please the gods

* It may be well to mention, that this scene contains allusions, extending through several lines, to the every-way luckless jailor's daughter. If I conceal the fact from you, you will, on finding it out for yourself, suspect that I consider it as making against my hypothesis, which assigns those episodical adventures to a different author from this scene. Be assured that I do not regard it in that light. It is plain that the underplot, however bad, has been worked up with much pains; and we can conceive that its author would have been loth to abandon it finally in the incomplete posture in which the fourth scene of this act left it. Ten lines in this scene sufficed to end the story, by relating the cure of the insane girl; and there can have been no difficulty in their introduction, even on my supposition of this scene being the work of the other author. If the two wrote at the same time, the poet who wrote the rest of the scene may have inserted them on the suggestion of the other; or if the drama afterwards came into the hands of that other, (which there seems some reason to believe,) he could easily insert them for himself. In any view these lines are no argument against my theory.

Sooner than such, to give us nectar with them,—
For we are more clear spirits! * *

2 *Knight.* Let us bid farewell;
And with our patience anger tottering fortune,
Who at her certain'st reels.

3 *Knight.* Come, who begins?

Palamon. Even he that led you to this banquet shall
Taste to you all. * *
* *
Adieu, and let my life be now as short
As my leave-taking. *(Lies on the block.)*

If we were in a situation to give due effect to the supernatural part of the story, the miserable end of Palamon would affect us with a mingled sense of pity and indignation. He has been promised success by the divinity whom he adored, and yet he lies vanquished with the uplifted axe glittering above his head. Both the drama and Chaucer's poem assume the existence of such feelings on our part, and hasten to remove the cause of them. A way is devised for reconciling the contending oracles; and the catastrophe which effects that end is in the old poet anxiously prepared by celestial agency.* Arcite has got the victory in the field, as his warlike divinity had promised him; and an evil spirit is raised for the purpose of bringing about his death, that the votary of the Queen of Love may be allowed to enjoy the gentler meed which his protectress had pledged herself to bestow. These supernal intrigues are in the play no more than hinted at in the way of metaphor.

A cry is heard for delay of the execution; Perithous rushes in, ascends the scaffold, and, raising Palamon from the block, announces the approaching death of Arcite, with nearly the same circumstances as in the poem. While he rode townwards from the lists, on a black steed which had been the gift of Emily, he had been thrown with violence, and now lies on the brink of dissolution. The speech which describes Arcite's misadven-

* The description which we have read of Mars's attributes reminds one strongly and directly of the fine speech in the poem, where old Saturn, the god of time, enumerates his own powers of destruction. It is far from unlikely that the one passage suggested the other. The rich can afford to borrow.

ture has been much noticed by the critics, and by some lavishly praised. With deference, I think it decidedly bad, but undeniably the work of Shakspeare. The whole manner of it is that of some of his long and over-laboured descriptions. It is full of illustration, infelicitous but not weak; in involvement of sentence and hardness of phrase no passage in the play comes so close to him; and there are traceable in one or two instances, not only his words, but the trains of thought in which he indulges elsewhere, especially the description of the horse, which closely resembles some spirited passages in the Venus and Adonis. It is needless to quote any part of this speech.

The after-part of this scene, which ends the play, contains some forcible and lofty reflection, and the language is exceedingly vigorous and weighty. In Chaucer the feelings of the dying Arcite are expressed at much length, and very touchingly; in the play they are dispatched shortly, and the attention continued on Palamon, who had been its previous object.

(Enter Theseus, Hippolita, Emilia, Arcite in a chair.)

Palamon. Oh, miserable end of our alliance!
The gods are mighty!—Arcite, if thy heart,
Thy worthy, manly heart, be yet unbroken,
Give me thy last words. I am Palamon,
One that yet loves thee dying.
Arcite. Take Emilia,
And with her all the world's joy. Reach thy hand:
Farewell! I've told my last hour. I was false,
But never treacherous: Forgive me, cousin!
One kiss from fair Emilia!—'Tis done:
Take her.—I die!
Palamon. Thy brave soul seek Elysium!

* * *

Theseus. *His part is played; and, though it were too short,*
He did it well. Your day is lengthened, and
The blissful dew of heaven does arrose you:
The powerful Venus well hath graced her altar,
And given you your love; our master Mars
Hath vouched his oracle, and to Arcite gave
The grace of the contention: So the deities
Have shewed due justice.—Bear this hence.
Palamon. Oh, cousin!
That we should things desire, which do cost us

The loss of our desire! that nought could buy
Dear love, but loss of dear love!

Theseus. * * * Palamon!
Your kinsman hath confessed, the right o' the lady
Did lie in you: for you first saw her, and
Even then proclaimed your fancy. He restored her
As your stolen jewel, and desired your spirit
To send him hence forgiven! The gods my justice
Take from my hand, and they themselves become
The executioners. Lead your lady off:
And call your lovers from the stage of death,
Whom I adopt my friends.—A day or two
Let us look sadly, and give grace unto
The funeral of Arcite, in whose end
The visages of bridegrooms we'll put on,
And smile with Palamon; for whom an hour,
But one hour since, I was as dearly sorry,
As glad of Arcite; and am now as glad,
As for him sorry.—Oh, you *heavenly charmers!*
What things you make of us! For what we lack,
We laugh; for what we have, are sorry still;
Are children in some kind.—Let us be thankful
For that which is, and with you leave disputes
That are above our question.—Let us go off,
And bear us like the time!

(*Exeunt omnes.*)

You have now before you an outline of the subject of this highly poetical drama, with specimens which may convey some notion of the manner in which the plan is executed. But detached extracts cannot furnish materials for a just decision as to the part which Shakspeare may have taken even in writing the scenes from which the quotations are given. If I addressed myself to one previously unacquainted with this drama, I should be compelled to request an attentive study of it from beginning to end. Such a perusal would convince the most sceptical mind that two authors were concerned in the work; it would be perceived that certain scenes are distinguished by certain prominent characters, while others present different and dissimilar features. If we are to assume that Fletcher wrote parts of the play, we must admit that many parts of it were written by another person, and we have only to inquire who that other was. Without recurring to any external presumptions whatever, I think there is enough in most or all of the parts which are evidently not Fletcher's, to appropriate them to the great poet whose name, in this instance, tradition has associated with his. Even in the passages which have been here selected, you cannot but have traced Shakspeare's hand frequently and unequivocally. The introductory views which I slightly suggested to your recollection, may have furnished some rules of judgment, and cleared away some obstacles from the path; and where I have failed in bringing out distinctly the real points of difference, your own acute judgment and delicate taste must have enabled you to draw instinctively those inferences which I have attempted to reach by systematic deduction.

In truth, a question of this sort is infinitely more easy of decision where Fletcher is the author against whose claims Shakspeare's are to be balanced, than it could be if the poet's supposed assistant were any other ancient English dramatist. If a drama were presented to us, where, as in some of Shakspeare's received works, he had taken up the ruder sketch of an older poet, and exerted his skill in altering and enlarging it, it would be very difficult indeed to discriminate between the original and his additions. He has often, especially in his earlier works, and in his histories more particularly, much of that exaggeration of ideas, and that strained and labouring force of expression, which marked the Hercules-like infancy of the English Drama. The stateliness with which Marlowe paces the tragic stage, and the magnificence of the train of solemn shews which attend him like the captives in a Roman procession of triumph, bear no distant likeness to the shape which Shakspeare's genius assumes in its most lofty moods. And with those also who followed the latter, or trode side by side with him, he has many points of resemblance or identity. Jonson has his seriousness of views, his singleness of purpose, his weight of style, and his "fulness and frequency of sentence;" Massinger has his comprehension of thought, giving birth to an involved and parenthetical mode of construction; and Middleton, if he possesses few of his other qualities, has much of his precision and straightforward earnestness of expression. In examining isolated passages with the view of ascertaining whether they were written by Shakspeare or by any of those other poets, we should frequently have no ground of decision but the insecure and narrow one of comparative excellence. When Fletcher is Shakspeare's only competitor, we are very seldom driven to adopt so doubtful a footing; we are not compelled to reason from difference in *degree*, because we are sensible of a striking dissimilarity in *kind*. We observe ease and elegance of expression opposed to energy and quaintness; brevity is met by dilation, and the obscurity which results from hurry of conception has to be compared with the vagueness proceeding from indistinctness of ideas; lowness, narrowness, and poverty of thought are contrasted with elevation, richness and comprehension: on the one hand is an intellect barely active enough to seek the true elements of the poetical, and on the other a mind which, seeing those finer relations at a glance, darts off in the wantonness of its luxuriant strength to discover qualities with which poetry is but ill fitted to deal; in the one poet we behold that comparative feebleness of fancy which willingly stoops to the correction of taste, and in the other, that warmth, splendour, and quickness of imagination, which flows on like the burning rivers from a volcano, quenching all paler lights in its spreading radiance, and destroying every barrier which would impede or direct its devouring course. You will remark that certain passages or scenes in this play are attributed to Shakspeare, not because they are superior to Fletcher's tone or manner, but because they are unlike it. It may be true that most of these possess higher excellence than Fletcher could have easily reached; but this is merely an extrinsic circumstance, and it is not upon it that the judgment is founded. These passages are recognized as Shakspeare's, not from possessing in a higher degree those qualities in which Fletcher's merit lies, but from exhibiting other qualities in which he is partially or wholly wanting, and which even singly, and still more when combined, constitute a style and manner opposite to his.

Indeed, since Fletcher is acknowledged to stand immeasurably lower than Shakspeare, the excellence of some passages might perhaps in itself be no unfair reason for refusing to the inferior poet the credit of their execution. But an analysis of the means by which the excellence is produced places us beyond the necessity of resorting, in the first instance at least, to this general ground of decision, which must, however, be taken into view, when we have been able to assume a position which entitles us to take advantage of it. In many parts of this play we find those external qualities which form Shakspeare's distinguishing characteristics, not separately and singly present, but combined most fully and most intimately; and it is consequently indisputable that we have, either Shakspeare's own writing, or a faithful and successful imitation of it. It is not easy to perceive with perfect clearness why it is that imitation of Shakspeare is peculiarly difficult; but every one is convinced that it is far more so than in the case of any other poet whatever. The range and opposition of his qualities, the rarity and loftiness of the most remarkable of these, and still more, the coincident operation of his most dissimilar powers, make it next to impossible, even in short and isolated passages, to produce an imitation which shall be mistaken for his original composition: but there is not even a possibility of success in an attempt to carry on such an imitation of him throughout many entire scenes. Where the external qualities of a work resemble his, the question of his authorship can be determined in no other way than by inquiring whether the essential elements, and the spirit which animates the whole, are his also; and that inquiry is not one for logical argument; it can be answered only by reflection on the effect which the work produces on our own minds. The dullest eye can discriminate the free motions of the living frame from the convulsed writhings which art may excite in the senseless corpse; the nightly traveller easily distinguishes between the red and earthy twinkling of the distant cottage-lamp, and the cold white gleam of the star which rises beyond it;—and with equal quickness and equal certainty the poetical sense can decide whether the living and ethereal principle of poetry is present, or only its corporeal clothing, its dead and inert resemblance. The emotion which poetry necessarily awakens in minds qualified as the subjects of its working, is the only evidence of its presence, and the measure and index of its strength. If we can read with coldness and indifference the drama which we are now examining, we must pronounce it to

4

be no more than a skilful imitation of Shakspeare ; but we must acknowledge it as an original if the heart burns and the fancy expands under its influence,—if we feel that the poetical and dramatic spirit breathes through all,—and if the mind bows down involuntarily before the powers of whose presence it is secretly but convincingly sensible. I cannot have a doubt that the parts of this work which I have pointed out as Shakspeare's will the more firmly endure this trial, the more closely and seriously they are revolved and studied.

The portions of the drama which, on such principles as these, have been set down as Shakspeare's, compose a large part of its bulk, and embrace most of the material circumstances of the story. They are,—the First Act wholly,—one scene out of six in the Third,—and the whole of the Fifth Act, (a very long one,) except one unimportant scene. These parts are not of equal excellence; but the grounds on which a decision as to their authorship rests, seem to be almost equally strong with regard to each. We have as yet been considering these scenes as so many separate pieces of poetry ; and they are valuable even in that light, not less from their intrinsic merit than as being the work of our greatest poet. If it be true merely that Shakspeare has here executed some portions of a plan which another had previously fixed on and sketched, the drama demands our zealous study, and is entitled to a place among Shakspeare's works. An examination of separate details cannot enable us to form any more specific opinion as to the part which he may have taken in its composition.

But there is a further inquiry on which we are bound to enter, whatever its result may be,—whether it shall allow us to attribute to Shakspeare a wider influence over the work, or compel us to limit his claim to the subsidiary authorship, which only we have yet been able to establish for him. We must now endeavour to trace the design of the work to its origin ; we must look on the parts in their relation to the whole, and investigate the qualities and character of that whole which the parts compose. Such an analysis is essential to an appreciation of the real merit of the drama, and suggests views of far greater interest than any which offer themselves in the examination of isolated passages. And it is likewise necessary as a part of the inquiry which is our object, not merely because it may tend to strengthen or modify the decisions which we have already formed, but because it will allow us to determine other important questions which we have had no opportunity of treating. It will justify us, if I mistake not, in pronouncing with some confidence, that this drama owes to Shakspeare much more than the composition of a few scenes,—that he was the poet who chose the story, and arranged the leading particulars of the method in which it is handled.

Before we enter the extensive and interesting field of inquiry thus opened to us, it may be well that I explain the reasons which seem distinctly to exclude from Shakspeare's part of the work one considerable portion of it,—the whole of the tragicomic under-plot. I have as yet assigned no ground of rejection but inferiority in the execution; but there are other reasons, which, when combined with that, remove all uncertainty. Slightly as this subordinate story has been described, enough has been said to point out remarkable imitations of Shakspeare, both in incident and character. The insane maiden is a copy of Ophelia, with features from Lear; the comments of the physician on her sickness of the mind, are borrowed in conception from Macbeth; the character of the fantastic schoolmaster is a repetition of the pedagogue in Love's Labour Lost; and the exhibition of the clowns which he directs, resembles scenes both in that play and in the Midsummer Night's Dream. All these circumstances together, or even one of them by itself, are enough to destroy the notion of Shakspeare's authorship. The likeness which is found elsewhere to Shakspeare's style, (and which is far closer in those other parts of the play than it is here,) is an argument, as I have shewn, in favour of his authorship; the likeness here in character and incident is even a stronger one against it. In neither of these latter particulars does Shakspeare imitate himself as he does in style. In some of his earlier plays indeed we may trace the rude outlines of characters, chiefly comic, which he was afterwards able to develope with greater distinctness and more striking features; but though the likeness, in those cases, were nearer and more frequent than it is, the transition from the rude block to the finished sculpture is the allowable and natural progress of genius. The bare reproduction of a figure or a scene already drawn with clearness and success, stands in a very different situation; and, even if it should be nearly equal to the original in actual merit, it creates a strong presumption of its being no more than the artifice of an imitator. Where the inferiority of execution is palpable, the doubt is raised into certainty. In the case before us, it is impossible to receive the idea of Shakspeare sitting down in cold blood to imitate the Ophelia, and to transfer all the tenderness of her situation to a new drama of a far lower tone, in which also it should occupy only a subordinate station. He could not have been guilty of this; he neither needed it, nor would have done it of free will; and, therefore, I could not have believed it to be his, though the execution had been far better than it is. But the inferiority is decided; the imitation produces neither vigour of style nor depth of feeling; in short, Shakspeare, if he had made the attempt, could not have failed so utterly. The comic parts are only subservient to the serious portion of this story; and if Shakspeare did not write the leading part, he was still less likely to have written the accessory; but, besides, the imitation is equally unsuccessful; and the original of the schoolmaster is said to have been a personal portrait, which was very unlikely to have been repeated by the first painter after the freshness of the jest was gone. I have been the more anxious to place in its true light the question as to this part of the drama, because on its seeming likeness to Shakspeare Steevens founds an ingenious hypothesis, by which he endeavours to account for the origin of the tradition as to Shakspeare's concern in the play. That this is a designed imitation of Shakspeare is abundantly clear; and it is not difficult to see why it is an unsuccessful one. Fletcher possesses much humour, but it is of a cast very unlike Shakspeare's, and very unfit to harmonise with it, or to qualify him for the imitation which he has here attempted. Why he made the attempt we shall be able to discover only when the freaks of caprice, and of poetical caprice, the wildest of all, shall be fully analyzed and fully accounted for. All that I have to prove is, that this portion of the work is not, and could not have been, Shakspeare's.

I have said that I consider as his both the selection of the plot, and much of its arrangement. As to the Choice of the Subject, my position is, that in this particular Shakspeare stands in unequivocal opposition to Jonson, Beaumont and Fletcher, and those others, contemporary with him, or a little his juniors, with whom his name is generally associated. I can easily shew that this opposition to the newer school in the choice of stories exists in Shakspeare individually; and this would be enough for my purpose; but I will go a little farther than I am called on, because I conceive him to share that opposition with some other poets, and because views open to us from this circumstance which are of some value for the right understanding of his characteristics. I say then, that in the choice of subjects particularly, as well as in other features, Shakspeare belongs to a school older than that of Fletcher, and radically different from it. The principle of the contrariety in the choice of subjects between the older and newer schools, is this: the older poets usually prefer stories with which their audience must have been previously familiar; the newer poets avoid such known subjects, and attempt to create an adventitious interest for their pieces, by appealing to the passion of curiosity, and feeding it with novelty of incident. The early writers may have adopted their rule of choice from a distrust in their own skill: but they are more likely to have been influenced by reflecting on the inexperience of their audience in theatrical exhibitions. By insisting on this quality in their plots, they hampered themselves much in the choice of them; and the subjects which offered themselves to the older among them, were mainly confined to two classes, history and the chivalrous tales, being the only two cycles of story with which, about the time of Shakspeare's birth, any general familiarity could be presumed. That such were the favourite themes of the infant English drama is abundantly clear even from the lists of old lost dramas which have been preserved to us. By the time when Shakspeare stepped into the arena, the zeal for translation had increased the stock of popular knowledge by the addition of the classical fables and the foreign modern novels; and his immediate precursors, some of whom were men of much learning, had especially availed themselves of the former class of plots. If, passing over Shakspeare, we glance at the plots of Fletcher, Jonson, or others of the same period, we find, among a great diversity of means, a search for novelty universally set on foot. Jonson is fond of inventing his plots; Beaumont and Fletcher usually borrow theirs: but neither by the former nor the latter were stories chosen which were familiar to the people, nor in any instance perhaps do they condescend to use plots which had been previously written on. Where Beaumont and Fletcher do avail themselves of common tales, they artfully combine them with others, and receive assistance from complexity of adventure in keeping their uniform purpose in view. The historical drama was regarded by the new school as a rude and obsolete form; and there are scarcely half a dozen instances in which any writer of that age, but Shakspeare, adopted it later than 1600. Historical subjects indeed wanted the coveted charm, as did also the Romantic and the Classical Tales, both of which shared in the neglect with which the Chronicles were treated. The Foreign Novels, and stories partly borrowed from them, or wholly invented, were almost the sole subjects of the newer drama, which has always the air of addressing itself to hearers possessing greater dramatic experience and more extended information than those who were in the view of the older writers.

Shakspeare, in point of time, stood between these two classes: does he decidedly belong to either, or shew a leaning, and to which? He unequivocally belongs to the older class; or rather, the opposition to the newer writers assumes in him a far more decided shape than in any of his immediate forerunners; for in them are found numerous exceptions to the rule, in him scarcely one. He returns, in fact, to more than one of the principles of the old school, which had begun in his time to fall into disuse. The external form of some of his plays, particularly his histories, is quite in the old taste. The narrative chorus is the most observable remnant of antiquity; and the long rhymed passages frequent in his earlier works, are abundant in the older writers: Peele uses them through whole scenes, and Marlowe likewise to excess. His continual introduction of those conventional characters, his favourite jesters, is another point of resemblance to the ruder stage. And his choice of subjects, when combined with the peculiarities of economy just noticed, as well as others, clearly appropriates him to the school of Lodge, Greene, and those elder writers who have left few works and fewer names. His Historical Plays are the perfection of the old school, the only valuable specimens of that class which it has produced, and the latest instance in which its example was followed; and he has had recourse to the Classical story for such subjects as approached most nearly to the nature of his English Chronicles. And you must take especial note, that, even in the class of subjects in which he seems to coincide with the new school,—I mean his Plots borrowed from Foreign Novels,—he assumes no more of conformity than its appearance, while the principle of contrariety is still retained. The new writers preferred untranslated novels, and, where they chose translated ones, disguised them till the features of the original were lost: Shakspeare not only uses translated tales—(this indeed from necessity)—and closely adheres to their minutest circumstances, but in almost every instance he has made choice of those among them which can be proved to have been most widely known and esteemed at the time. Most of his plots founded on fanciful subjects, whether derived from novels or other sources, can be shewn to have been previously familiar to the people. The story of Measure for Measure had been previously told; that of As you Like It, he might have had from either of two popular collections of tales; the fable of Much Ado about Nothing seems to have been widely spread, and those of All's Well That Ends Well, and the Winter's Tale; Romeo and Juliet appears in at least one collection of English novels, and in a poem which enjoyed much popularity. These are sufficient as examples; but a still more remarkable circumstance is this. In repeated instances, about twelve in all, Shakspeare has chosen subjects on which plays had been previously written; nay more, on the subjects which he has so re-written, he has produced some of his best dramas, and one his very masterpiece. Julius Cesar belongs to this list; *Lear* does so likewise; and HAMLET. Is not that a singular fact? I can use it at present only as a most valuable proof that the view which I take is an accurate one. But Shakspeare has also, oftener than once, applied to the chivalrous class of subjects, which was exclusively peculiar to the older school. Its tales indeed bore a strong likeness to his own most esteemed subjects of study; for, amidst all their extravagancies and inconsistencies, the Gothic romances and poems, the older of them at all events, professed in form to be chronicles of fact, and in principle to assume historical truth as their groundwork. Pericles is founded on one of the most popular romances of the middle ages, which had been also versified by Gower, the second father of the English poetical school. The characters in The Midsummer Night's Dream are classical, but the costume is strictly Gothic, and shews that it was through the medium of romance that he drew the knowledge of them; and the Troilus and Cressida presents another classical and chivalrous subject, which Chaucer had handled at great length, also invested with the richness of the romantic garb and decoration.

Fletcher and Shakspeare being thus opposed to each other in their choice of subjects, what qualities are there in the Plot of The Two Noble Kinsmen, which may appropriate the choice of it to either? In the first place, it is a chivalrous subject,—a classical story which had already been told in the Gothic style. The nature of the story then could have been no recommendation of it to Fletcher. He has not a single other subject of the sort; he has even written one play in ridicule of chivalrous observances, and the sarcasm of that humorous piece,* both in the general design and the particular references, is aimed solely at the prose romances of knight-errantry, a diseased and posthumous off-shoot from the parent-root, whose legitimate and ancient offspring, the metrical chronicles and tales, he seems neither to have known nor cared for. Secondly, this story must have been unacceptable to Fletcher, because it was a fa-

* The Knight of the Burning Pestle.

miliar one in England. This fact is perhaps sufficiently proved by its being the subject of that animated and admirable poem of Chaucer, which Dryden has pronounced little inferior to the Iliad or Æneid; but it is still more distinctly shewn by a third fact, which completely clenches the argument against Fletcher's choice of it as a subject. No fewer than two plays had been written on this story before the end of the sixteenth century; the earlier of the two, the Palamon and Arcite of Edwards, acted in 1566, and printed in 1585, and another play called by the same name, brought on the stage in 1594.*

It is thus, I think, proved almost to demonstration, that the person who chose this subject was not Fletcher; and what has been already said, even without the specific evidence of individual passages, creates a strong probability that the choice was made by Shakspeare rather than by any other dramatic poet of his time. If the question be merely one between the two writers,—if, assuming it to be proved that Shakspeare wrote parts of the play, we have only to ask which of the two it was that chose the subject,—we can surely be at no loss to decide. But the presumption in Shakspeare's favour may be elevated almost into absolute certainty, while, at the same time, some important qualities of his will be illustrated,—if we inquire what was the real extent to which he attached himself to the study of the chivalrous poetry, from which this subject is taken, and the influence which that study was likely to have had, and did actually exercise on his writings.

If, being told that a dramatic poet was born in England in the latter half of the sixteenth century, whose studies, for all effectual benefit which they could have afforded him, were limited to his own tongue, we were asked to say what course his acquisitions were likely to have taken, our reply would be ready and unhesitating. English literature was of narrow extent before the time in question, and, according to the invariable progress of mental culture, had been evolved first in those finer branches which issue primarily from the ima-

* Weber's Beaumont and Fletcher. Henslowe MSS. published by Malone:—Boswell's Shakspeare, vol. iii. p. 303.

gination and affections, and appeal for their effect to the principles in which they have their source. Poetry had reached a vigorous youth, history was in its infancy, philosophy had not come into being. Had the field of study been wider, it was to poetry in an especial manner that a poet had to betake himself for an experience and skill in his art, and in the language which was to be its instrument. And it was almost solely to the narrative poets that Shakspeare had to appeal for aid and guidance; for preceding writers in the dramatic walk could teach him little. They could serve as beacons only and not examples, and he had to search in other mines for the materials to rear his palace of thought. But the English poetical writers who preceded him are all more or less impressed with the seal of the Gothic school, and the most noted among them belong to it essentially. Chaucer, Lydgate, and Gower, to more than one of whom Shakspeare is materially indebted, were the heads of a sect whose subjects and form of composition were varied only as the various forms and subjects of the foreign romantic writers. The rhymed romance, the metrical vision, the sustained allegorical narrative or dialogue, were but differing results of the same principle, and forms too of its original developement; for Britain was the mother and nurse of much of the finest chivalrous poetry, as well as the scene where some of its most fascinating tales are laid. It is true that English poetry before the time of Elizabeth presents but few distinguished names; but there is a world of unappropriated treasures of the chivalrous class of poetry, which are still the delight of those who possess the key to their secret chambers, and were the archetypes of the earlier poets of that prolific age. It is important to recollect, that among the poets who adorn that epoch, the narrative preceded the dramatic. Spenser belongs, in every view, to the romantic or Gothic school; the heroic Mort d'Arthur was the rule of his poetical faith; and it was that school, headed by him, which Shakspeare, on commencing his course and choosing his path, found in possession of all the popularity of the day. Every thing proves that he allowed himself to be guided by the prevailing taste. His early poems belong in design to Spenser's school, and their style is often imitative of his. In his dramas he has many points of resemblance to the older chivalrous poets, besides his occasional adoption of their subjects. His respect for Gower is shewn by the repeated introduction of his shade as the speaker in his chorusses; and particular allusions and images, borrowed from Gothic usages and chivalrous facts, occur at the first blush to the recollection of every one. But there is a more widely spread influence than all this. Many of his most faulty peculiarities are directly drawn from this source, and his innumerable misrepresentations or mistakes are not so truly the fruit of his own ignorance, as the necessary qualities of the class of poets to which he belonged, shared with him by some of the greatest poetical names which modern Europe can cite. In this situation are indeed almost all the irregularities and anomalies which have furnished the unbelievers in the divinity of his genius with objects of contemptuous abuse;—his creation of geographies wholly fictitious,—his anachronisms in facts and customs,—his misstatements of historical detail,—his dukes and kings in republics,—his harbours in the heart of continents, and his journies over land to remote islands,—his heathenism in Christian lands and times, and his bishops, and priests, and masses, *in partibus infidelium*. We may censure him for these irregularities if we will; but it is incumbent on us to recollect that Chaucer and Spenser must bear the same sentence: and if the faults are considered so weighty as to shut out from our notice the works in which they are found, the early literature, not of our own country only, but of the whole of continental Europe, must be thrown aside as one mass of unworthy fable.

In truth Shakspeare, in throwing himself on a style of thought and a track of study which exposed him to such errors, did no more than retire towards those principles which not only were the sources of poetry in his own country, but are the fountains from which, in every nation, her first draughts of inspiration are drunk. Poetry in its earlier stages is universally neither more nor less than a falsifying of history. The decoration of the Real is an exertion of the fancy which marks an age elder than the creation of the purely Ideal; it is an effort more successful than the attempt which follows it, and the wholly fictitious has always the appearance of being resorted to from necessity rather than choice. Cathay is an older and fitter seat of romance than Utopia; and the historical paladins and soldans are characters more poetical than the creatures of pure imagination who displaced them. But this walk of poetry is one in which she never can permanently linger: her citadel indeed is real existence partially comprehended, but she is unable to defend the fortress after knowledge has begun to sap its outworks; she needs ignorance for her ally while she occupies the domain of history, and when that companion deserts her, she unwillingly retreats on the Possible and Invented, where she has no enemy to contest her possession of the ground.—While however she does continue in her older haunt, she must sometimes wander out of her imperfectly defined path, and her errors will depend, both in kind and in amount, on the amount and kind of her knowledge. That the qualities of poetical literature, in every nation, are dependent on the number and species of those experiences from which in each particular case the art receives its materials, is indeed too evident to need illustration; but some curious inferences are deducible from an application of this truth to the contrast which is found between the poetical literature of modern Europe, and that older school which has been called the classical. The inherent excellencies of the ancient Greek poetry may yet remain to be accounted for from other causes; but this one principle was adequate to produce the most distinguishing qualities of the pagan literature, while it is distinctly the very same principle, acting in different circumstances, which has given birth to the opposite character of the modern school of invention. During the period which witnessed the gradual rise of that anomalous fabric of poetry, from whose prostrate fragments the perfected literature of Christian Europe has been erected, knowledge (I am uttering no paradox) was of vast extent; it embraced many different ages and many distant regions: but it was also universally imperfect; much was known in part, but nothing wholly. Hence proceeded the specific difference of that widely-spread form of poetical invention, namely, the superabundance and incongruity of attributes with which it invested historical truth ; and it is not very difficult to discover why many of those attributes have never thoroughly amalgamated with the principal mass. The various sources from which the materials of the romantic poetry were drawn, present themselves at once to every mind. By the peculiar state of their knowledge, and the rude activity of spirit which was its consequence, the early poets of modern Europe were prepared to invent a species of literature which should be strictly national in its subjects, and in its essential parts wholly original. That new branch was exposed, however, to modifications of various kinds. One temptation to introduce foreign elements, by which its authors were assailed, was singularly strong, and can scarcely in any other instance have operated on a literature arising in circumstances otherwise so favourable to originality, as those in which they were placed. That temptation was offered by the imperfect acquaintance with the classical authors which formed one part of their scattered and ill-reconciled knowledge. They were influenced by this cause, as they could not have failed to be ; and the representations of feelings, habits, and thought, which they borrowed from this source, being in their nature dissimilar to the constituent parts of the system to which they were adjected, never could have harmonised with these, and, under any circumstances, must have always continued to be excrescences. Other elements of the new system were naturally neither evil in themselves, nor inconsistent with the principles with which it was attempted to combine them, but have assumed the aspect of deformity and incongruity solely from incidental and extraneous causes. The fictions and mistakes which the ignorance of those fathers of our modern poetical learning superinduced on history ancient and modern, and on every thing which related to the then existing state either of the material world or of human society, were allowable ornaments, so long as knowledge afterwards acquired did not stamp on them the brand of falsehood ; but the moment that the falsity was exposed, and the charm of possible existence broken, those adjuncts lost their empire over the imagination, and with it their appearance of fitness as materials for mental activity. In supernatural invention, the early romantic poets were still more unfortunate ; for when they endeavoured to colour with imaginary hues the awful outlines of the true faith, they attempted a conjunction of holiness with impurity, an identification of the spirit with the flesh, a marriage between the living and the dead ; the purer essence revolted from the union, and the human mind could acquiesce in imagining it only while it remained bound in the darkness and fetters of religious corruption. Turn now to the Grecian poetry, and mark how closely the same principles have operated on it, although the difference of the circumstances has made the result different. The first Grecian inventors were, it is true, protected in a great measure from the influence of any foreign literature, simply by the ignorant rudeness of those ages of the world during which their task was performed ; and even here I have no doubt that an influence not very dissimilar did actually operate ; for there seems to be good reason for supposing that, if we had before us the wild songs of such bards as the Thracian Orpheus, or the old Musæus, we should find them strongly marked by that orientalism towards which the later Greek poetry which remains to us betrays so continual a tendency. In other respects, the spirit in which the Greeks formed their poetical system was identical with our own. Their elder poets falsified historical facts, invented or disguised historical characters, and framed erroneous representations of the past in time and the distant in place, no otherwise than did the romantic fabulists ; and the classical inventors continued to have sufficient faith placed in their fictions, merely because knowledge advanced too slowly to allow detection of their falsity so long as the literature of the nation continued to exist for it as a present possession. With their religious belief, again, every attractive invention harmonised, and every splendid addition was readily incorporated as a consistent part ; where all was false, a falsity the more was unperceived or uncensured, and where sublimity and beauty were almost the only objects sought, they were gladly accepted from whatever quarter or in whatever shape they came.

So far as these considerations seem to elucidate the principles on which Shakspeare proceeded, they do so by exhibiting him as withdrawing from his own times as to his subjects and the external form of his works, though not as to their animating spirit, —as placing himself delightedly amidst the rude greatness of older poetry and past ages, and viewing life and nature from their covert, as if he had sat within a solitary and ruined aboriginal temple, and looked out upon the valley and the mountains from among those broken and massive columns, whose aspect gave majesty and solemnity to the landscape which was beheld through their moss-grown vistas. So far as these views have any force as a defence of faults detected in the great poet, that defence is founded on the consideration that the errors were unavoidable consequences of the system which produced so much that was admirable, and that they were shared with him by those whom he followed in his selection of subjects and form of writing. So far as all that has been said on this head has a close application to the main subject of our inquiry, its sum is briefly this. An argument arises in favour of Shakspeare's choice of the plot of this drama, from its general qualities, as a familiar and favourite story, and one of a class which had been frequently used by the older dramatists; that argument receives additional strength from the fact of this individual subject having been previously treated in a dramatic form; and it is rendered almost impregnable when we consider the subject particularly as a chivalrous story, and as belonging and leading us back to that native school to which Shakspeare, though in certain respects infected by the exotic taste of the age, yet in essentials belonged,—the wilderness in which Chaucer had opened up the well-head of poetry, where Gower and Lydgate had drunk freely, and Sackville had more sparingly dipped his brow,—the paradise through which Spenser had joyfully wandered with the heavenly Una,—the patriarchal forest into which afterwards Milton loved to retire from his lamp-lighted chamber, to sleep at the foot of some huge over-hanging oak, and dream of mailed knights riding by his resting-place, or fairy choirs dancing on the green hillocks around,—the enchanted rose-garden where Shakspeare himself gathered those garlands of beauty, which he has described as adding glory even to his thoughts of love.

When in the chronicle of wasted time
I see description of the fairest wights,
And beauty making beautiful old rhyme
In praise of ladies dead and lovely knights;
Then in the blazon of sweet beauty's best,
Of hand, of foot, of lip, of eye, of brow,
I see this antique pen would have expressed
Even such a beauty as you master now.

Sonnet 106.

In the Arrangement of the Plot also there are circumstances which point emphatically to Shakspeare's agency. One strong argument is furnished by a very prominent quality of the plot as it is managed,—its simplicity. This quality is like him, as being in this case the result of a close adherence to the original story; but it is also like him in itself, since the arrangement of all his works indicates the operation of a principle tending to produce it, namely, a reliance for dramatic effect on the execution of the parts rather than on the mechanical perfection or complication of the whole. His contemporaries, in their own several ways, bestowed extreme care on their plots. With Beaumont and Fletcher, hurry, surprise, and rapid and romantic revolution of incident are the main object, rather than tragic strength or even stage effect: their plays would furnish materials for extended novels, and are often borrowed from such without concentration or omission. Shakspeare's comparative poverty of plot is not approached by them even in their serious plays, and the lively stir of their comic adventures is the farthest from it imaginable. Jonson's plots are constructed most elaborately and admirably: one or two of them are without equal for skill of conduct and pertinency and connection of parts. That cautious and industrious poet never confided in his own capability of making up for feebleness of plan by the force of individual passages; and his distrust was well judged, for the abstract coldness of his mind betrays itself in every page of his dialogue, and his scenes need all their beauty of outline to conceal the frigidity of their filling up. Ford and Massinger agree much in their choice of plots, both preferring incidents of a powerfully tragic nature: but their modes of management are widely different. Ford, on the gloom of whose stories glimpses of pathos fall like moonlight, delights when he comes to work up the details of his tragic plan, in softening it down into the most dissolving tenderness; at his bidding tears flow in situations where we listen rather to hear Agony shriek, or look to behold Terror freezing into stone; his emotion is not the rising vehemence of present passion, but the anguish, subsiding into regret, which lingers when suffering is past, and suggests ideas of eventual resignation and repose;—his verse is like the voice of a child weeping itself to sleep. Massinger crowds adventure upon adventure, and his situations are wound up to the height of unmixed horror: for stage effect and tragic intensity, some of them, as for example the last scene in The Unnatural Combat, and the celebrated one in The Duke of Milan, are unequalled in the modern drama, and worthy of the sternness of the antique; but it is in the design alone that the tragic spirit works; the colouring of the details is cold as monumental marble; the pomp of lofty eloquence apes the simplicity of grief, or silence is left to interpret alike for sorrow or despair. To the carefulness in outlining the plan and devising situations, thus shewn in different ways, Shakspeare's manner is perfectly alien. He never exhausts himself in framing his plots, but reserves his strength for the great aim which he had before him, the evolution of human character and passion, a result which he relied on his own power to produce from any plot however naked. He does not want variety of adventure in many of his plays; but he has it only where his novel or chronicle gave it to him: he does not reject it when it is offered, but does not make the smallest exertion to search for it. Some of his plays, especially his comedies, have actually no plot, and those, too, the very dramas in which his genius has gained some of its most mighty victories. The Tempest is an instance: what is there in it? A ship's company are driven by wreck upon an island; they find an old man there who had been injured by certain of them, and a reconciliation takes place. The only action of As You Like It is pedestrian; if the characters had been placed in the forest in the first scene, the drama would have been then as ripe for its catastrophe as it is in the last. The Midsummer Night's Dream relates a midnight stroll in a wood; and the unreal nature of the incidents is playfully indicated in its name. It is from no stronger materials than those three frail threads of narrative that our poet has spun unrivalled tissues of novel thought and divine fancy. And, as in his lighter works he is careless of variety of adventure, so in his tragic plays he does not seek to heap horrors or griefs one upon another in devising the arrangement of his plots. In this latter class of his works, the skill and force with which the interest is woven out of the details of story and elements of character, make it difficult for us to see how far it is that we are indebted to these for the power which the scene exerts over us. But with a little reflection we are able to discover, that there is scarcely one drama of his, in which, from the same materials, situations could not have been formed, which should have possessed in their mere outline a tenfold amount of interest and tragic effect to those which Shakspeare has presented to us. Hamlet offers, especially in the two last acts, some remarkable proofs of his indifference to the means which he held in his hands for increasing the tragic interest of his situations, and of the boldness with which he threw himself on his own resources for the creation of the most intense effect out of the slenderest outline. But no example can shew more strikingly his independence of tragic situation, and his power of concocting dramatic power out of the most meagre elements of story, than the third act of the Othello. It contains no more than the developement and triumph of the devilish design which was afterwards to issue in murder and remorse ; and other writers would have treated it in no other style than as necessary to prepare the way for the harrowing conclusion. In the Moor's dialogues with Iago, the act of vengeance, ever and anon sternly contemplated, and darkening all with its horror, is yet but one ingredient in the misery of the tale. These scenes are a tragedy in themselves, the story of the most hideous revolution in a noble nature ; and their catastrophe of wretchedness is complete when the tumult of doubt sinks into resolved and desolate conviction,—when the Moor dashes Desdemona from him, and rushes out in uncontrollable agony.—Read also the conclusion of Lear, and learn the same lesson from the economy of that most touching scene. The horrors which have gathered so thickly throughout the last act, are carefully removed to the back-ground, and free room is left for the sorrowful groupe on which every eye is turned. The situation is simple in the extreme; but how tragically moving are the internal convulsions for the representation of which the poet has worthily husbanded his force! Lear enters with frantic cries, bearing the body of his dead daughter in his arms; he alternates between agitating doubts and wishful unbelief of her death, and piteously experiments on the lifeless corpse; he bends over her with the dotage of an old man's affection, and calls to mind the soft lowness of her voice, till he fancies he can hear its murmurs. Then succeeds the dreadful torpor of despairing insanity, during which he receives the most cruel tidings with apathy, or replies to them with wild incoherence; and the heart flows forth at the close with its last burst of love, only to break in the vehemence of its emotion,—commencing with the tenderness of regret, swelling into choking grief, and at last, when the eye catches the tokens of mortality in the dead, snapping the chords of life in a paroxysm of agonised horror.

> Oh, thou wilt come no more;
> Never, never, never, never, never!
> —Pray you, undo this button: Thank you, Sir.—
> Do you see this?—*Look on her—look*—HER LIPS!
> *Look there! Look there!*

The application here of the differences thus pointed out is easy enough. Fletcher either would not have chosen so bare a story, or he would have treated it in another guise. The incidents which constitute the story are neither many nor highly wrought: they are only the capture of the two knights,—their becoming enamoured of the lady,—the combat which was to decide their title to her,—and the death of Arcite after it. And no complexity of minor adventures is inserted to disturb the simplicity so presented. In all this there is nothing which Fletcher could have found sufficient to maintain that continuity and stretch of interest which he always thought necessary. He would have invented accessory circumstances, he would have produced new characters, or thrust the less important personages who now fill the stage, further into the foreground, and more constantly into action: the one simple and inartificial story which we have, possessing none of his mercurial activity of motion, and scarcely exciting a feeling of curiosity, would have been transformed into a complication of intrigues, amidst which the figures who occupy the centre of the piece as it stands, would have been only individuals sharing their importance with others, and scarcely allowed room enough to make their features at all distinguishable.

In the management of particular scenes of this play, likewise, certain circumstances are observable, which, separately, seem to go a certain length in establishing Shakspeare's claim to the arrangement, and have considerable force when taken together. The second scene of the first act would appear to have been sketched by him rather than Fletcher, from its containing no activity of incident, and serving no obvious purpose but the developement of the character and situation of the two princes; a mode of preparation not at all practised by Fletcher. Neither does any consequence flow from the beautiful scene immediately following; a circumstance which points out Shakspeare as having arranged the scene, and would strengthen the evidence of his having written the dialogue, if that required any corroboration. The bareness and undiversified iteration of situation in the first three scenes of the last act form one presumption against the devising of those scenes by Fletcher. The economy of the fifth scene of that act, in which Emilia, left alone on the stage, listens to the noise of the combat, is also, to me, strongly indicative of Shakspeare. The contrivance is unusual, but extremely well imagined. I do not recollect an instance in Fletcher bearing the smallest likeness to it, or founded on any principles at all analogous to that which is here called into operation. In Shakspeare I think we may, in more than one drama, discover something which might have given the germ of it. He has not only in his historical plays again and again regretted the insufficiency of the means possessed by his stage, or any other, for the representation of such spectacles; but in several of those plays he has devised expedients for avoiding them. In Henry V. we have the battle of Azincour; but the only encounter of the opposite parties is that of Pistol and the luckless Signor Dew. In the first part of Henry IV. he has shewn an unwillingness to risk the effect even of a single combat; for in the last scene of that play, where prince Henry engages Hotspur, the spectator's attention is distracted from the fight between them, by the entrance of Douglas, and his attack on the prudent Falstaff. In Richard II. the lists are exhibited for the duel of Bolingbroke and Norfolk, which is inartificially broken off at the very last instant by the mandate of the king. But a more deeply marked likeness to the spirit in which the scene in The Two Noble Kinsmen is arranged, meets us in Lady Macbeth watching and listening while her husband perpetrates the murder, like a bad angel which delays its flight only till it be assured that the whispered temptation has done its work. And in this combat scene, even the ancient and artless expedient used, of relating important events by messengers brought in for that sole end, and having no part in the action, may be noticed as belonging to an older form of the drama than Fletcher's, and as being very frequently practised by Shakspeare himself.

In quitting our cursory examination of the qualities which distinguish the mechanical arrangement of the play, we may advert to the mode in which those influences are conceived which give motion to the incidents of the story, and regulate its progress. The dramatic art is a representation of human character in action; and action in human life is prompted by passion, which the other powers of the mind serve only to guide, to modify, or to quell. In the conception of the passions which are chiefly operative in this drama, there seems to be much that is characteristic of a greater poet than Fletcher. In the first place, the passions which primarily originate the action of the piece are simple; they are Love and Jealousy; the purest and most disinterested form of the one, and the noblest and most generous which could be chosen for the other. The conception is Shakspeare's in its loftiness and magnanimity; and it is his also as being a direct appeal to common sympathies, modified but slightly by partial or fugitive views of nature. But it also resembles him in the singleness and coherence of design with which the idea is seized and followed out. It cannot be necessary that I should specifically exemplify the closeness with which those ruling passions are brought to bear on the leading circumstances of the story from first to last. And it is almost equally superfluous to remind you how far any such adherence to that unity of impulse operates as evidence in a question between the two poets whom we have here to compare. Fletcher, in common with other poets of all ranks inferior to the highest, is unable to preserve any one form of passion or of character skilfully in the foreground: he may seem occasionally to have proposed to himself the prosecution of such an end, but he either degenerates into the exhibition of a few over-wrought dramatic contrasts, or loses his way altogether amidst the complicated adventures with which he incumbers his stories. This inability to keep sight of an uniform design is in truth one striking argument of inferiority; and the clearness with which Shakspeare conceives a definite purpose, and the fixedness with which he pursues it, go very far to unravel the great secret of his power. I have already pointed out to you, perhaps without necessity, wherein it is that his strength of passion consists; that it is not in the incidents of his fable, but in his mode of treating the incidents; that he will not rely on mere vigour or skill of outline in his stage-grouping, for that influence which he is conscious of being always able to acquire more worthily, by the beauty and emotion which he breathes into the organic formation of the living statuary of the scene; that he refuses to sacrifice to the meretricious attraction of strained situations or entangled incidents, the internal and self-supporting strength of his historical pictures of the heart, or the unflinching accuracy of his demonstrations of the intellectual anatomy. In a similar way you will look for his unity of purpose, not in the mechanical economy of his plots, but in the elementary conception of his characters, and in his developement of the principles of passion under whose suggestions those characters act. He chooses as the subject of his delineation some mightily and truly conceived impersonation of human attributes, inconsistent it may be in itself, but faithful to its prototype as being inconsistent according to the rules which guide inconsistency in our enigmatical mental constitution; for the exhibition of the character so imagined he devises some chain of events by which its internal springs of action may be brought into play; and he traces the motion and results of those spiritual impulses with an undeviating steadiness of design, which turns aside neither to raise curiosity nor to gratify a craving for any other mean· excitement. Some singular instances of Shakspeare's fine judgment in clinging to one great design, are furnished by the Othello. The death of Desdemona has been compared with the murder of Annabella, a scene (evidently drawn from it) in a drama of Ford's on a story which makes the flesh creep. Some have pronounced Ford's scene superior in pathos to Shakspeare's: I think it is decidedly so. The tender mournfulness of the language and few images is exquisite, and the sweet sad monotonous melody of the versification is indescribably affecting. Is it from weakness that Shakspeare has not given to the death of his gentle lady an equally strong impress of pathos? No. He was not indeed susceptible of the feminine abandonment of Ford; but he was equal to a manly tone of feeling, fitted to excite a truer sympathy. He has refused to stretch the chords of feeling to the utmost in favour of Desdemona; and his refusal has a design and meaning in it. There is anguish in the scene, and the most utter yielding to overpowering sorrow; but it is the Moor who feels those emotions, and it is the exhibition of his mind which is the leading end of this scene, as of the rest of the drama. The suffering lady is but an inferior actor in the scene; her situation is brought out with perfect skill and genuine tenderness, so far as it is consistent with the first object and illustrative of it; but its expression is arrested at the point where its further developement would have marred the effect of the scene as a whole, and broken in on its pervading spirit. Ford had no such aim in view; and the very scene of his which is so beautiful in itself, loses almost all its force when regarded as a part of the play in which it is inserted.

These principles of Shakspeare's could be traced as influencing the drama of the Two Noble Kinsmen, even if there were nothing farther to shew their effect than what has been already noticed. But their power is displayed still more admirably in a second quality in the mode of conception, less open to notice, but breathing actively through all. There is skill in the mental machinery which gives motion to the story; but there is even greater art in the application of a hidden influence, which controls the action of the moving power, and equalizes its effects. That secret principle is Friendship, the operation of which is shewn most distinctly in the Kinsmen, guiding every part of their behaviour except where their mutual claim to Emilia's love comes into operation, never extinct even there, though its effect be sometimes suspended, and awakening on the approach of Arcite's death, with a warmth which is natural as well as touching. But this feeling has a farther working: Love of Friends is in truth the leading idea of the piece: the whole drama is one sacrifice on the altar of one of the holiest influences which affect the mind of man. Palamon and Arcite are the first who bow down before the shrine, but Theseus and Perithous follow, and Emilia and her sister do homage likewise. This singular harmony of parts was an idea perfectly beyond Fletcher's reach; and the execution of it was equally unfit for his attempting. The discrimination, the delicate relief, with which the different shades of the affection are elaborated, is inimitable. The love of the Princesses does not issue in action; it is a placid feeling, which gladly contemplates its own likeness in others, or turns back with memory to the vanished hours of childhood: with Theseus and his friend the passion is exhibited dimly, as longing for exertion, but not gifted with opportunity; and in the Kinsmen, it bursts out into full activity, quelling all but the one omnipotent passion, and tempering and purifying even it. With this exception you will not look for much of Shakspeare's skill in delineating character. The features of the two Princes are aptly enough distinguished; but neither in them nor in any of the others is there an approach to his higher efforts. You will recollect that in his acknowledged works those finer and deeper pryings into character have place only in few instances; and that the greater number of his dramas depend for their effect chiefly on other causes, some of which are energetic in this very play.

While you successively inspected particular passages in this play, your attention was necessarily called both to the character of its imaginative portions, and to the tone of reflection which is so frequently assumed in it. The drama having been now put entirely before you, I shall wish you to ponder its ruling temper as a whole, and to determine whether that temper is Fletcher's, or belongs to a more thoughtful, inquisitive, and solemn mind. When you institute such a reconsideration, I shall be desirous that you contemplate the internal spirit of the work from a loftier and more commanding station than that which you formerly occupied; and I shall crave you to view its elements of thought and feeling less as the qualities of a literary work, than as the signs and results of the mental constitution of its author. I cannot regard as altogether foreign to our leading purpose any inquiry which may hold out the promise of illustrating the characteristics of Shakspeare even slightly, and of teaching us to mingle a more active discernment in the reverence with which we look up to the Star of Poets from the common level of our unendowed humanity. You will therefore have the patience to accompany me in the suggestion of some queries as to the character of his mode of thinking, and the way in which his reflective spirit and his poetical qualities of mind are combined and influence each other. We may be able to perceive the more distinctly the real character both of his intellect and his poetical faculty, if you will consent that our investigation shall set out from a point which you may be inclined to consider somewhat more remote than is altogether necessary. It is to be desired that we should have clearly in our view, first, the true functions of the poetical faculty, and, secondly, the province in poetical invention which legitimately belongs to the imagination, properly so called. Sound conclusions on both these points are indispensible to sound criticism on individual specimens of the poetical art; and when we attempt to reason on particular cases without having those conclusions placed prominently in view at the outset, the vagueness of ordinary language makes us constantly liable to lose sight of their true grounds and distinctions. The laying down of such principles at the institution of an enquiry into the poetical character of a great poet, is therefore in no degree less useful than the inculcating of familiar truths is in the instructions of religious and moral teachers; the end in each of the cases being, not the establishing of new principles, but the placing of known and admitted ones in an aspect which shall render them influential; and the necessity in each arising from the danger which exists, lest the principles, acknowledged in the abstract, should in practice be wholly disregarded.

We can in no way discover the real character and objects of the Poetical Art so easily as by contrasting it with the Arts of Design; and the materials for such a comparison are afforded by the Laocoon of Lessing. The principles established in that admirable essay will scarcely be now disputed, and may be fairly enough summed up in the following manner.*—A study of the Grecian works of art convinces us, that "among the ancients Beauty was the presiding law of those arts which are occupied with Form;" that to that supreme object the Greek artists sacrificed every collateral end which might be inconsistent with it; and that, in particular, they expressed the external signs of mental commotion and bodily suffering to no farther extent than that which allowed Beauty to be completely preserved. Now, that this subordination of Expression to Beauty is a fundamental principle of art, and not a mere accidental quality of Grecian art individually, is proved by considering the peculiar constitution and mechanical necessities of art. Its representations are confined to a single instant of time; and that one circumstance imposes on it two limitations, which necessarily produce the characteristic quality of the Grecian works. First, "the expression must never be selected from what may be called the *acme* or transcendent point of the action;" and that because, the power of the arts of design being confined to the arresting of a single point in the developement of an action, it is indispensible that they should select a point which is in the highest degree significant, and most fully excites the imagination; a condition

* It would be unfair not to state, that I quote and refer to the translation of the Laocoon published by Mr. De Quincey, in Blackwood's Magazine for November 1826; and that I am not otherwise acquainted with that or any other work of Lessing.

which is fulfilled only by those points in an action in which the action moves onward, and the passion which prompts it increases; and which is not fulfilled in any degree by the highest stage of the passion and the completion of the action. Secondly, a limitation is imposed as to the choice of the proper point in the onward progress of the action: for art invests with a motionless and unchanging permanence the point of action which it selects; and consequently any appearance which essentially possesses the character of suddenness and evanescence is unfit to be its subject, since the mind cannot readily conceive such transitory appearances as stiffened into that monumental stability.—Since it is by the limitation of the Fine Arts to the representation of a single instant of time that the two limitations in point of expression are imposed, and since Poetry is not subject to that mechanical limitation, but can describe successively every stage of an action, and every phasis of a passion, it follows that this latter art is not fettered by the limitation in expression, which is consequent on the physical limitation of the other; and hence the exhibition of passion in its height is as allowable in poetry as it is inadmissible in the arts of design. And since the whole range and the whole strength of human thought, action, and passion, are thus left open to the poet as subjects of his representation, it follows likewise, that Beauty "can never be more than one amongst many resources, (and those the slightest), by which he has it in his power to engage our interest for his characters."

It will be remarked, that the purport of Lessing's reasoning, so far as he has in express terms carried it, is no more than to demonstrate the important truth, that the Fine Arts are confined by certain limits to which Poetry is not subject. His elucidation of the principles of poetry is purely incidental and negative. His reasoning seems however necessarily to infer certain further consequences, the examination of which has a tendency to cast additional light on the true end and character of the poetical art; and it is for this reason, rather than from any difficulty lying in the way of those implied results, that I wish now to direct your notice to their nature, and the grounds on which their soundness rests. Lessing's second canon does not assume the arts of design as pursuing any further end than their original and obvious one, the Representation of Form: it simply directs that only those appearances of form shall be represented which admit of being conceived as permanent. And as the feelings which art desires to awaken are pleasurable, and as forms considered merely *as* forms give pleasure only when they are beautiful, Art would thus be regarded as proposing for its object nothing beyond a Representation of the Beautiful, and Verisimilitude in that representation. The first rule of limitation however implies a great deal more: it looks to forms, not as such, but as tokens significant of certain qualities not inherent in their own nature; for the quality which it requires to be possessed by works of art, is a capability of exciting the imagination to frame for itself representations of human action and passion; and in this view, those feelings which the qualities of form considered as such are calculated to arouse, are no more than an accidental part of the impression which the representation makes. It appears, therefore, that art *may* pursue two different ends,—the excitement of the feeling which Beauty inspires, and the excitement of the feeling which has its root in human Sympathy; and the question at once occurs,—Is each of these purposes of art equally a part of its original and proper province? Or, since it is sufficiently clear that the effects which the last mentioned canon contemplates as produced by the fine arts, are effects which are also produced by poetry, (whether its sole effects or not, it is immaterial to this question to settle), the question may be put in another form:—Is it to be believed, that the arts of design, which have admittedly for one purpose the reproduction of the Beautiful in form, have also as an equally proper and original purpose the framing of representations of form calculated to affect the mind with feelings different from the feeling of the Beautiful,—these feelings being identically the same with those which are at least the most obvious effects of poetry? Reasons crowd in upon the mind, evincing that the question must be answered by an unqualified negative. The production of poetical effects cannot have been an *original* purpose of the fine arts, which certainly were brought into existence by the love of Beauty; and the production of those effects is plainly also an exertion in which the fine arts overstep their limits, and wander into the region which belongs of right to the poetical art, and to it alone. That Expression in painting and sculpture is an extraneous and borrowed quality, is made almost undeniably evident by this one consideration, that it requires, as we have seen, to be always kept subdued, and allowed to enter only partially into the composition of the work. And, again, it is no argument against that position, to say that the strongest and most general interest and admiration are excited by those works of art in which expression is permitted to go the utmost length which the physical limits of the art permit. For the universality of this preference only proves, that the feelings of our common humanity influence more minds than does the pure love of the beautiful; and the greater strength of the feeling produced by expression only evinces that poetry, which works its effect by means of that quality, is a more powerful engine than the sister-art for stirring up the depths of our nature. And it may be quite true that those works of art which confine themselves to the attempt to move the calmer feeling due to Beauty, are the truest to their own nature and proper aim, although an endeavour to unite with that the attainment of higher purposes may be admissible, and in some instances highly successful. I apprehend that although an art should propose as its main end the production of one particular effect, it does not follow that its effects should be confined to the production of that alone, if its physical conditions permit the partial pursuit of others. More especially, if an art should admit of uniting to a certain extent with its own peculiar and legitimate end the prosecution of another loftier than the first, surely we might expect to find such an art occasionally taking advantage of the license; and yet its doing so would not compel us to say, that both these are its proper and original purposes. And the fact is, that the attempt is seldom made; for very few works of classical art exist in which the union of the two principles is tried, the end sought being usually the representation of beauty, and that alone. In no way, however, can the radical difference and opposition between the two qualities be evinced so satisfactorily as by a comparison of the effects which they severally produce on the mind. Expression, the poetical element, gives rise to a peculiar activity of the soul, a certain species of reflective emotion, which, it is true, is easily distinguishable from underived passion, and does not necessarily produce like it a tendency to action, but which yet essentially partakes of the character of mental commotion, and is opposed to the idea of mental inactivity. The feeling which Beauty awakens is of a character entirely opposite. The contemplation of the Beautiful begets an inclination to repose, a stillness and luxurious absorption of every mental faculty: thought is dormant, and even sensation is scarcely followed by the perception which is its usual consequence. It is with this softness and relaxation of mind that we are inspired when we look on such works as the Venus de Medici, in which beauty is sole and supreme, and expression is permitted to be no farther present than as it is necessary as an indication of the internal influence of soul, that so those sympathies may be awakened, without whose partial action even beauty itself possesses no power. If we turn to those few works of ancient art, in which the opposite element is admitted, we are conscious that the soul is differently acted upon, and we may be able by reflection to disentangle the ravelled threads of feeling, and distinguish the mental changes which flow upon and through each other like the successive waves on the sea-beach. In contemplating the Apollo, for instance, a feeling akin to the poetical, or rather identical with it, is awakened by the divine majesty of the statue; and upon the quiet and self-brooding luxury with which the heart is filled by the perfect beauty of the youthful outlines, there steals a more fervent emotion which makes us proud to look on the proud figure, which makes us stand more erect while we gaze, and imitate involuntarily that godlike attitude and expression of calm and beautiful disdain. Or look to the wonderful Laocoon, in which the abstract feeling of beauty is even more deeply merged in the human feeling of the pathetic,—that extraordinary groupe, in which continued meditation arouses more and more actively the emotion of sympathy, while we view the dark and swimming shadows of the eyes, the absorbed and motionless agony of the mouth, and the tense torture of the iron muscles of the body. It is impossible to conceive that an art can propose to itself, as originally and properly its own, two ends so difficult of reconcilement and so different in the qualities by which they are brought about. Finally, the Plastic Arts offer form directly to the sense of sight, whereas it is very doubtful whether poetry can convey, even indirectly, any visual image. Consequently, the result of admitting Expression as a primary and legitimate end of the arts of form, would be to ascribe to them an innate and underived capability of presenting directly to the senses both beauty and the wide circle of human action and feeling; while the genius of Poetry, by her nature shut out from direct representation of the beautiful, whose shadows she can evoke only through the agency of associated ideas, would have even her own kingdom of thought and passion, her power as the great interpreter of mind, shared with her by a rival whom the decision would acknowledge indeed as possessing a right to the divided empire, but who is disqualified by the nature of her instruments from exercising that sovereignty to the full. And, on the other hand, by the acknowledgment that the arts of form are not properly a representation of human action or human passion, and that when they aim at becoming so, they attempt a task which is above and beyond their sphere, and in which their success can never be more than partial, Poetry is exhibited in an august and noble aspect, as stooping to lend a share in her broad and lofty dominion to another art of narrower scope, which is so enabled to gain over the mind an influence transcending its own unassisted capacities.

If you shall be able to think this excursive disquisition justifiable, it will be because it insensibly leads us to perceive what truly is the legitimate and sole end of the Poetical Art, and because it thus clears the way for one or two elementary propositions regarding the functions of the Poetical Faculty. First, we perceive that poetry does not aim at the representation of visual beauty. I do not say that beauty may not form the subject of poetry: my meaning is, that the poet can depict it poetically in no way except by indicating its effects on the mind. When poetry mistakingly attempts to represent beauty by its external form, its failure to affect the mind is signal and complete, and must be so, even supposing it to be possible that the picture should be so full and accurate that the painter might sketch from it. The reason of this is perhaps discoverable. Such a description cannot affect the mind with the poetical sentiment, because it does not represent to the imagination those qualities by which it is that the poetical effect is produced; and if it were to move the mind at all, it must be with those feelings which beauty excites when it is seen corporeally present. It fails to operate even this effect, and why? Beauty of form affects the mind through the intervention of sense; and the perception of the sensible qualities of form is followed instantaneously and necessarily by the pleasurable emotion. This mental process is involuntary, and the nature of the sentiment excited implies inactivity and absorption of the mind. When however the imagination is called on to combine into a connected whole the scattered features which words successively present, an effort of the will is necessary: and the failure in the pleasurable effect appears to be adequately accounted for (independently of any imperfection in the result of the combination) by the inconsistency of this degree of mental activity with the inert frame of mind which is requisite for the actual contemplation and enjoyment of the beautiful. When, again, the poet represents beauty in the method chalked out for him by the nature of his art, it is quite impossible that he can convey any distinct visual image; for he represents the poetical qualities by indicating them as the causes which produce some particular temper or frame of mind: and as every mind has its distinctive differences of association, a truly poetical picture is not realised by any two minds with precisely similar features. And the mood of mind to which this representation gives birth is radically opposite to the other; it is active, sympathetic, and even reflective: we seem, as it were, to share the feeling with others, to derive an added delight from witnessing the manner in which they are affected, or even to have the original passive sentiment of pleasure entirely swallowed up in that energetic emotion.* Secondly, the true subject of poetry is

* The theory which, denying to the Beautiful any capacity of giving pleasure through its innate qualities, ascribes its effects exclusively to

Mind. Its most strictly original purpose is that of imaging mind *directly*, by the representation of humanity as acting, thinking, or suffering; it presents images of external nature only because the weakness of the mind compels it; and it is careful to represent sensible images solely as they are acted on by mind. When it makes the description of external nature its professed end, it in truth does not represent the sensible objects themselves, but only exhibits certain modes of thought and feeling, and characterises the sensible forms no farther than as the causes which produce them. Thirdly, The most characteristic function of the poetical faculty is *analytical*; it is essentially a *perception*, a power of discovery, analysis, and discrimination. An object having been presented to it by the imagination, it discovers, and separates from the mass of its qualities, those of them which are calculated to affect the mind with that emotion which is the instrumental end of poetry; coincidently with the perception and discovery of the qualities, it perceives and experiences the peculiar effect which each particular quality produces; and, lastly, it sets forth and represents those resulting moods of mind, indicating at the same time what those qualities of the object are through which they are excited. Its task of combination is no more than consequent on this process, and supposes each step of it to have been previously gone through. Fourthly, It follows, (and this is the result which makes the inquiry important), that the poetical faculty is measured by the strength and accuracy with which it perceives the poetical qualities of those objects which the imagination suggests as its materials, and not by the number of the ideas so presented. A forgetfulness of this truth has occasioned more misapprehension and

the associated ideas which the contemplation of it calls up, proceeds wholly on the assumption, that the sentiment awakened by beauty when it is beheld bodily present, is the same with that which flows from a poetical description of it. If it be true (as I must believe it is,) that the feelings in the two cases are essentially different, the hypothesis falls to the ground. Its maintainers seem in truth to have drawn their conclusions altogether from reflection on the effects produced by Beauty when it is represented in poetry, where association is undoubtedly the source of the enjoyment; and an attention to the working of the fine arts would have taught other inferences.

false criticism than any other error whatever; and we are continually in danger of the mistake, from the extension of meaning which use has attached to the word imagination, that term being commonly employed to designate the poetical faculty. This extended application is perhaps unavoidable; but it is on that account the more necessary to guard against the misconception always likely to arise from the original signification of the word, which we can never discard entirely from the mind in using it in a secondary sense.—You do not need to be reminded how completely the history of the poetical art evinces, that these positions, whether expressly acquiesced in or not, have been invariably acted on in the judgments which the world has pronounced in particular cases. The inadequacy of a representation of forms by their external attributes to constitute poetical pictures, could be instanced from every bad poem which has ever been written; and the great truth, that the external world is exhibited poetically only by being represented as the exciting cause of mental changes, has been illustrated in no age so singularly as in our own. The writings of Wordsworth in particular have stretched the principle to the utmost extent which it can possibly sustain; demanding a belief that all external objects are poetical, because all can interest the human mind; establishing the reasonableness of the assumption by the boldest confidence in the strength and delicacy with which the poetical perception can trace the qualities which awaken that interest, and the progress of the feeling itself; and applying the poetical faculty to the transforming of every object of sense into an energetic, and as it were sentient existence. And attention is especially due to the decision which has always recognized, as the rule of poetical excellence, the operation of some power independent of mere wealth of imagination, ranking this latter quality as one of the lowest merits of poetry. We are apt to forget that those minds whose conceptions have been the most strongly and truly poetical, are by no means those whose poetical ideas have been the most abundant; that an overflow of poetical images has been coincident with an intense perception of their most efficient poetical relations only in a few rare instances; and that it is precisely where the highest elements of the poetical are most active that the imagination is usually found to offer the fewest images as the materials on which the poetical faculty should work. It is enough to name Dante, or, a still more singular instance, Alfieri. In both cases the poetical influence rests on the intensity of the one simple aspect of grandeur or passion in which a character is presented, and in both that simplicity is unrelieved and undecorated by any fulness of imagery.*

These fundamental principles of the poetical art possess a closer application to Dramatic Poetry than to any other species. All poetry being directly or indirectly a representation of human character; and human character admitting of appreciation only by an exhibition of its results in action; and action being prompted by the passionate impulses of the mind, which its reflective faculties only modify or stay; it follows that the Passions are the leading subjects of Poetry, which consequently must be examined in the first instance with a view to its strength and accuracy as a representation of the working and results of that department of the mind. The nature of the dramatic art allows this rule to be applied to it with the greatest strictness. The drama is the species which presents the essential qualities of poetry less mingled with foreign adjuncts than they are in any other species; and there seems to be a cause, (independent of its mechanical necessities), enabling it to dispense with those decorations which abound in other kinds of poetry. The acted drama presents its picture of life directly to the senses, and permits the imagination, without any previous exertion, to proceed at once to its proper task of forming its own combinations from the sensible forms thus offered to it; and even when the drama is read, the office of the imagination in representing to itself the action and the characters of the piece, is an easy one, and performed without the necessity of great activity of mind. On the other hand, in the epic, or any other species of poetry which represents action by

* Alfieri appears to have himself perceived accurately wherein it is that his power lies, when he says, with his usual self-reliance: "Se la parola invenzione in tragedia si restringe al trattare soltanto soggetti non prima trattati, nessuno autore ha inventato meno di me." "Se poi la parola invenzione si estende fino al *far cosa nuova di cosa già fatta*, io son costretto a credere che nessuno autore abbia inventato piu di me."

words, and not by an imitation of the action itself, the imagination has at first to form, from the successively presented features of the poetical description, a picture which shall be the exciting cause of the poetical impression : this supposes considerable energy of thought, and the necessity of relief from that exertion seems to have suggested the introduction of images of external nature and the like, on which the fancy may rest and disport itself. Those classes of poetry which are either partially or wholly didactic, cannot receive a strict application of the principles of the pure art; because they are not properly poetry, but attempts to make poetical forms serve purposes which are not poetical.

Our journey has at length conducted us to Shakspeare, of many of whose peculiar qualities we have been gaining scattered glimpses in our progress. We remark him adopting that species of poetry which, necessarily confined by its forms, is yet the noblest offspring of the poetical faculty, and the truest to the purposes of the poetical art, because it is the most faithful and impressive image of the mind and state of man. We find him seated like an eastern sovereign amidst those who have adopted this highest form of poetry; and we cannot be contented that, in reverentially acknowledging his worthiness to fill the throne, we should render him only a hasty and undiscerning homage. A discrimination of the particular qualities by which his sway is mainly supported, is rendered the more necessary by that extraordinary union of qualities, which has made him what he is, the unapproached and the unapproachable.—We are accustomed to lavish commendations on his vast Imagination. Before we can perceive what rank this quality of his deserves to hold in an estimate of his character, we must understand precisely what the quality is which we mean to praise. If the term used denotes merely the abundance of his illustrative conceptions, it expresses what is a singular quality, especially as co-existent with so many other endowments, but useful only as furnishing materials for the use of the poetical power. If the word is meant to call attention to the strength and delicacy with which his mind grasps and embodies the poetical relations of those overflowing conceptions, (still considered simply as illustrative or decorative), the quality indicated is a rare and valuable gift, and is especially to be noted in an attempt to trace a likeness to his manner. Still however it is but a secondary ground of desert; it is even imperfectly suited for developement in dramatic dialogue, and it frequently tempts him to quit the genuine spirit and temper of his scene. If, again, in speaking of the great poet's imagination, we have regard to the poetical character of many of his leading conceptions, to the ideal grandeur or terror of some of his preternatural characters, or even to the romantic loveliness which he has thrown, like the golden curtains of the morning, over the youth and love of woman,—we point out a quality which is admirable in itself, and almost divine in its union with others so opposite, a quality to which we are glad to turn for repose from the more severe portions of his works,—but still an excellence which is not the most marked feature of his character, and which he could want without losing the essential portion of his identity. We could conceive, (although the idea is sacrilege to the genius and the altar of poetry,) we could conceive that The Tempest had remained unwritten, that Miranda had not made inexperience beautiful by the spell of innocence and youth, that the hideous slave Caliban had never scowled and cursed, nor Ariel alighted on the world like a shooting-star,—we could dismiss alike from our memories the moon-light forest in which the Fairy Court revel, and the lurid and spectre-peopled ghastliness of the cave of Hecate,—we could in fancy remove from the gallery of the poet's art the picture which exhibits the two self-destroyed lovers lying side by side in the tomb of the Capulets,—and we could discard from our minds, and hold as never having been invented by the poet, all which we find in his works, possessing a character similar to these scenes and figures;—and yet we should leave behind that which would support Shakspeare as having pursued the highest ends of his art, and as having attained those ends more fully than any other who ever followed them: Richard would still be his; Macbeth would think and tremble, and Lear weep and be mad; and Hamlet would still pore over the riddle of life, and find in death the solution of its mystery. If it is to such characters as these last that we refer when we speak of the poet's power of imagination, and if we wish to designate by the word the force with which he throws himself into the conception of those characters, then we apprehend truly what the sphere is in which his greatness lies, although we either describe the whole of a most complicated mental process by naming a single step of it, or load the name of that one mental act with a weight of meaning which it is unfit to bear.

It is here, in his mode of dealing with human character, that Shakspeare's supremacy confessedly lies; and the conclusions which we have reached as to the great purpose of poetry, allow us easily to perceive how excellence in this department justifies the universal decision, which places at the summit of poetical art the poet who is pre-eminently distinguished by it. What is there in Shakspeare's view of human character which entitles him to this high praise? His truth of painting is usually specified as the source of his strength; in what sense is he true to nature? Is that faithfulness to nature consistent with any exercise of the imagination in the representation of character? And how? And again, bow does his reflective temper of mind harmonize with or arise out of the view of human life which he takes?

Poetry, as we have seen, and dramatic poetry more strictly than any other species, must be judged primarily as a representation of passion and feeling; and when it is defective as such, it has failed in its proper end. Its prosecution of that end, however, is subject to two important limitations. First, if it is to be in any sense a *true* representation of human action, it must represent human nature not partially, but entirely; it must exhibit not only the moving influences which produce action, but also the counteracting forces which in real life always control it. It must be a mirror of the intellectual part of the human mind, as well as of the passionate. Secondly, if, possessing the first requisite, truth, it is to be also an *impressive* representation, (that is, such a representation as shall effect the ends of poetical art,) it must set up an ideal and elevated standard to regulate its choice of the class of intellectual endowment which is to form the foundation of the characters which it portrays. We discover the cause of Jonson's inferiority in his failure in obedience to the latter of these rules, though he scrupulously complied with the first: we discover the prevailing defect of all the other dramatic writers of that period, to consist in their neglect even of the first and subsidiary rule, which involved a complete disregard to the other.—These latter have, as well as Shakspeare, been proposed as models, from their close imitation of nature. The merit of truth to nature belongs to them only in a very confined sense. They seize one oblique and partial aspect of human character, and represent it as giving a true and direct view of the whole; they are the poets of the passions, and no more; they have failed to shadow forth that control which the calmer principles of our nature always exert over the active propensities. Their excellence consequently is to be looked for only in scenes which properly admit the force of unchecked passion, or of passions conflicting with each other; and in those scenes where the more thoughtful spirit ought to work, we must be prepared to meet either exaggeration of feeling or feebleness of thought, either the operation of an evil principle, or, at best, a defect of the good one. Even in their passionate scenes, the vigour of the drawing is the merit oftener than the faithfulness of the portrait; they delight to figure the human mind as in a state of delirium, with the restraining forces taken off, and the passions and the imagination boiling, as if the brain were maddened by opiates or fever. Fierce and exciting visions come across the soul in such a paroxysm; and in the intensity of its stimulated perceptions, it gazes down into the abysses of nature, with a profound though transitory quickness of penetration. It is a high merit to have exhibited those partial views of nature, or even this exaggerated phasis of the mind; and the praise is shared by no dramatic school whatever; (for the qualities of the ancient are different;) but it must not be assumed that the drama fulfils its highest purposes, by representations so partial, so distorted, or so disproportioned. As these poets of impulse bestowed no part of their attention on the intellect in any view, they produced their peculiar effect, such as it was, without any attempt at that higher task of selection and elevation in intellectual character for which the universality of views which they wanted must always serve as the foundation. They had accordingly little scope for the due introduction of reflection in their works; and their turn of mind inclined them little to search for it when it did not naturally present itself.—Jonson resembled Shakspeare in wideness of aim; he is most unlike him in the method which he adopted in the pursuit of his end. The two stood alone in their age and class, as alone aiming at truth to nature in any sense; both wished to read each of the opposite sides of the scroll of human character: but the one read correctly the difficult writing in which intellectual character is traced, while the other misapprehended and misinterpreted its meaning, and even allowed the eagerness with which he perused this perplexing page, to withdraw his attention from the more easy meaning of the other. The fault of his characters as intellectual beings, is that they are individuals and no more; faithful or grotesque portraits of reality, they are not touched with that purple light which affords insight into universal relations and hidden causes. His failure is shewn by its effect: his characters are not so conceived as to lead the mind to the comprehension of any thing beyond their own individual peculiarities, or to elevate it into that region of active and conceptive contemplation into which it is raised by the finest class of poetry: he exhibited reality as reality, and not in its relation to possibility; he even diverges into the investigation of causes, instead of seeing them at a glance, and indicating them by effects; he anatomised human life, and hung up its dry bones along the walls of his study.

In the close obedience which Shakspeare rendered to each of these two canons, borne in upon his mind by the instantaneous suggestions of his happy genius, we may discover the origin of his tremendous power. To commence at the point where his adherence to the first and subsidiary rule is most slightly manifested, it is to be noticed, that his works are marked throughout by a predominance of the qualities of the understanding over the fancy and the passions. This is not true of the fundamental conception of the work, nor of the relations by which his characters are united into the dramatic groupes; in these particulars the poetical faculty is allowed to work freely: but it is after the initial steps have been taken under her guidance, that the rule is committed to the sterner power of intellect. The stir of fancy often breaks through the restraints which hold it in check; the warmth of feeling effervesces very unfrequently. The poet's personages are all more or less marked by an air of quiet sense, which is extremely unusual in poetry, and incompatible with the unnecessary or frequent display of feeling; and accordingly, his less important scenes, whether they be gay or serious, occupied in the business of the drama, or devoted to an exchange of witty sallies, possess, where they aim at nothing higher, at least a degree of intellectual shrewdness, which very often savours of worldly coldness. Viewed merely as increasing the effect of his passionate scenes, this prevailing sobriety of tone gives him an incalculable advantage: passion in his works bursts out when it is let loose, like the spring of a mastiff unchained. It is of this quality, his sober rationality, that we are apt to think when we acknowledge his truth of representation; and the excellence is indispensible to truth in any sense, because the want of it gives birth to imperfection and distortion of views; but I apprehend that it is to his aiming at a higher purpose that we have to look for the genuine source of his power. While we mark the gradual rise of the intellectual element of poetical character upwards from its lowest stage, we are in truth approximating to a rule which issues in something beyond a bare and unselected reproduction of reality. Poetry aims at representing the whole of man's nature; and yet a picture of human character, embracing all its features, but neither skilfully selecting its aspect, nor majestically combining its component parts, would not effect the ends of poetry: for that art contemplates not individual but general truth, not that which is really produced, but that which may be conceived without doing violence to acknowledged principles; instead of presenting a bare portraiture of mental changes, it exhibits them in an aspect which teaches their relation to the system of universal nature; it is seemingly conversant with facts, but it imperceptibly hints at causes; it aims at exciting the imagination to frame pictures for itself, and for that reason, if for no other, it must be permitted to idealize and ennoble the individual realities from which its materials are collected. The mode in which poetry affects the mind is illustrated by the description which we read of a certain ancient painting. That piece represented a young soldier surrounded by several enemies and desperately defending himself; but his own figure alone was admitted into the field of view, and the motions and place of his unseen enemies were indicated solely by the life, energy, and significance of the attitude in which he was drawn. Shakspeare's attachment to truth of representation never tempted him to forget the true purpose of his art. While he is true to nature by attempting the treatment of his whole subject, he is true to it in the manner and with the restrictions which the nature of poetry requires: he is true to principles which admit of being conceived as producing effects, not to effects individually observed as resulting; the creatures of his conception possess no qualities which unfit them for exciting the mind as poetical character should excite it; they are not repulsive by the unexampled and unatoned-for congregation of evil qualities, not mean by the absence of lofty thought, not devoid of poetical significance by confining the imagination to the qualities by which they are individually marked. You will particularly remark, that, while he had to bring out the features of his characters by subjecting them to tragic and calamitous events, he was careful not to figure them as unsusceptible of the influence of those external evils. The lofty view which he took of human nature did indeed admit the idea of a resistance to calamity, and a triumph over it, based on internal and conscious grandeur; but this is an aspect in which he does not present the human mind; the stoical Brutus is the only character in which he has attempted such a conception, which he has there developed but partially. But while he was contented, even in his noblest characters, to represent passion in all its strength and directed towards its usual objects, he had open to him sources of tragic strength unknown to those poets who describe passion only. Where passion alone is represented, no spectacle is so agitating as the conflict of contending passions; and the narrowness of such views of nature permits that tragic opposition to be no further exhibited. Shakspeare had before him a wider field of contrast—the conflict between the passions and the reason—a struggle between powers inspired with deadly animosity, and each, as he conceived them, possessed of gigantic strength. He has worthily represented that terrible encounter, engaging every principle and faculty of the soul, and shaking the whole kingdom of man's being with internal convulsions. It is in such representations that his power is mainly felt; and his pictures are at the same time truest to nature and most faithful to the ends of tragic art, by the subjugation of the intellectual principle which is the catastrophe of the strife. The reason is assaulted by calamity from without, and borne down by an host of rebellious feelings attacking it internally. It is to the delineation of such characters as afford scope for this exhibition of mental commotion that Shakspeare has especially attached himself: the thoughtful and reflective in character is at once his favourite resort, and the field of his triumph.

The poet's selection of the intellectual and reflective in character, as the subject of his art, is thus indicated as his guiding principle, to whose operation all other principles and rules are but subservient. The reflective element however is in excess with Shakspeare, and its undue prevalence is not destitute of harmony with the principle which produces its legitimately moderated effects. He is a Gnomic Poet; and he is so, because he is emphatically the poet of man. He pauses, he reflects, he aphorizes; because, looking on life and death as he looked on them, viewing the nature of man from so lofty a station and with a power of vision so far-reaching, so acute, and so delicate, it was impossible but the deepest solemnity of meditation should diffuse itself through all the chambers of his soul. His enunciations of general truth are often serious and elevated even in his gayer works; and where the scene denied him an opportunity of introducing these in strict accordance with the business of the drama, he makes his personages, as it were, step out of the groupe, to meditate on the meanings of the scene, to hold a delicately implied communication with the spectator, and to hint the general maxims and principles which lurk beneath the tragic and passionate shews. He has gone beyond this: he has brought on the stage characters whose sole task is meditation, whose sole purpose in the drama is the suggesting of high and serious reflection. Jaques is the perfection of such a character; and the office which he discharges bears more than a fanciful likeness in conception to the task of the ancient chorus. That forgotten appendage of the Grecian drama originated indeed from incidental causes; but, being continued as a part of the dramatic plan, it had a momentous duty assigned to it: it suggested, it interpreted, it sympathised, it gave the key-note to the reflections of the audience. A profound sense of the highest purposes and responsibilities of the art prompted this employment of the choral songs; and no way dissimilar was the impression which dictated to Shakspeare the introduction of the philosophically cynical lover of nature in that one play, and the breaks of reflection so frequent with him in many others.—It is worthy of remark, that this spirit of penetrating thought, ranging from every-day wisdom to philosophical abstraction, never becomes morose or discontented. Man is a selfish being, but not a malignant one; yet the acts resulting from the two dispositions are often very similar, and it is the error of the misanthrope to mistake the one for the other. Shakspeare's well-balanced mind was in no danger of this mistake: his keen-sightedness often makes him sarcastic, but the sarcasm forced on a mind which contrasts the poorness of reality with the splendours of imagination, is of a different temper from that which is bred from lowness of thought and fretful envy. Shakspeare has devoted one admirable drama to the exhibition of the misanthropic spirit, as produced by wrongs in a noble heart; but the sternness which is the master-note of that work is softened by the most beautiful intervals of redeeming tenderness and good feeling. The only work of his evidently written in ill humour with mankind, is the Troilus, which, both in idea and execution, is the most bitter of satires.

The application of the distinctive qualities of Shakspeare's tone of thought to the spirit of The Two Noble Kinsmen, is a task for your own judgment and discrimination, and would not be aided by suggestions of mine. I have stated the result to which I have been led by such an application; and I am confident that you will be able to reach the same conclusion by a path which may be shorter than any which I could clear for you. In connexion however with this inquiry, I would direct your attion to one other truth possessing a clear application here. Shakspeare's thoughtfulness goes the length of becoming a Moral distinction and excellence. That such a difference does exist between Shakspeare and Fletcher, is denied by no one; and the moral tone of this play, in those parts which I have ventured to call Shakspeare's, is distinctly a higher one than Fletcher's. It is uniform and pure, though the moral inquisition is less severe than Shakspeare's often is. If Massinger or Jonson had been the poet alleged to have written part or the whole of the work, it would have been difficult to draw any inference from this circumstance by itself; but when the question is only between Shakspeare and Fletcher, even an abstinence from gross violation or utter concealment of moral truth is an important element in the decision; and the positively high strain here maintained is a very strong argument in favour of the purer writer.

I am tempted, however, to carry you somewhat further on this head, because I must confess that I cannot see the grounds on which Johnson and others have rested their sweeping condemnation of Shakspeare's morality. There is, it must be admitted, much to blame, but there is also something worthy of praise; and praise on this score is what Shakspeare has scarcely ever received. He has been charged with licentiousness, and justly; but even in this particular there are some circumstances of palliation, besides the equivocal plea of universal example, and the doubt which exists whether most of his grosser dialogues are not interpolations. Mere coarseness of language may offend the taste, and yet be so used as to give no foundation for any heavier charge. There surely never was a mind which could receive one evil suggestion from the language wrung from the agonized Othello. Even where this excuse does not hold, Shakspeare preserves one most important distinction quite unknown to his contemporaries. By them looseness of dialogue is introduced indifferently anywhere in the play, licentiousness of incident is admitted in any part of the plot, and debauchery of life is attributed without scruple to those persons in whom interest is chiefly meant to be excited. It may be safely stated that Shakspeare almost invariably follows a rule exactly opposite. His inferior characters may be sometimes gross and sensual; his principal personages scarcely ever are so: these he refuses to degrade needlessly, by attributing to them that carelessness of moral restraint of which Fletcher's men of pleasure are so usually guilty. There are only two plays in which he has violated this rule, exclusively of some unguarded expressions elsewhere.

But the language which has been held on this question would lead us to believe that his guilt extends further,—that he is totally insensible to any moral distinctions, and blind to moral aims and influences. Of most dramatic writers of his time this charge is too true. Their characters act because they will, not because they ought,—for happiness, and not from duty: the lowness of their aim may be disguised, but it is inherent, and cannot be eradicated. We might read every work of Fletcher's without discovering (if we were ignorant of the fact before) that there exists for man any principle of action loftier in its origin than his earthly nature, or more extended in its object than the life which that nature enjoys. But nothing of this is true as to Shakspeare. That his morality is of the loftiest sort cannot be asserted. He does not, like Milton, look out on life at intervals from the windows of his sequestered hermitage, only to turn away from the sight and indulge in the most fervent aspirations after immortal purity, and the deepest adoration of uncreated power; nor does he grovel in the dust with that ascetic humiliation and religious sense of guilt which overcame the strong spirit of Michel Angelo. But he shares much of the solemnity of moral feeling which possesses all great minds, though in him its influence was restrained by external causes. He moves in the hurried pageant of the world, and sometimes wants leisure to moralize the spectacle; and even when he does pause to meditate, the world often hangs about his heart, and he thinks of life as men in action are apt to think of it. But moral truth, seldom lost sight of, is never misrepresented: evil is always described as being evil: the great moral rule, though often stated as inoperative, is always acknowledged as binding. Read carefully any of his more lofty tragedies, and ponder the general truths there so lavishly scattered; and you will find that an immense proportion of those apophthegms have a moral bearing, often a most solemn and impressive one. Even in his lighter plays there is much of the same spirit: in all he is often thoughtful, and he is never long thoughtful without becoming morally didactic. This is much in any poet, and especially in a dramatist, who exhibits humanity directly as active, and is under continual temptations to forget what action tempts men to forget in real life. His neglect of duly distributing punishment and reward is no moral fault, so long as moral truth is kept sight of in characterizing actions, while that neglect is borrowed closely from reality. And the same thing is true of his craving wish for describing human guilt, and darkening even his fairest characters with the shadows of weakness and sin. The poetry which depicts man in action is then unfortunately truest when it represents him as most deeply enslaved by the evil powers which surround him. Different poets have proceeded to different lengths in the degree of influence which they have assigned to the evil principle: most have feared to draw wholly aside the veil which imagination always struggles to keep before the nakedness of man's breast; and Shakspeare, by tearing away the curtain with a harsher hand, has but enabled himself to add a tremendously impressive element of truth to the likeness which his portrait otherwise bears to the original. His view of our state and nature is often painful; but it is its reality that makes it so; and he would have wanted one of his strongest holds on our hearts if he had probed them less profoundly; it is by his unflinching scrutiny of mortal infirmity that he has forged the very strongest chain which binds us to his footstool. He reverences human nature where it deserves respect: he knows man's divinity of mind, and harbours and expresses the loftiest of those hopes which haunt the heart like recollections: he represents worthily and well the struggle between good and evil, but he feared to represent the better principle as victorious: he had looked on life till observation became prophetical, and he could not fable that as existing which he sorrowfully saw could never be. The milk of human kindness in the bosom of Macbeth is turned to venom by the breath of an embodied fiend; the tempered nobility and gentleness of the Moor are made the craters through which his evil passions blaze out like central fires; and in the wonderful Hamlet, hate to the guilty pollutes the abhorrence of the crime,—irresolution waits on consciousness,—and the misery of doubt clings to the solemnity of meditation. This is an awful representation of the human soul; but is it not a true one? The sibylline volume of man's history is open before us, and every page of it is written in blood or tears. And not only are such views of human fate the truest, but they are those which are most fitted to arouse the mind to serious, to lofty, even to religious contemplation,—to guide it to the fountains of moral truth,—to lead it to meditations on the dark foundations of our being,—to direct its gaze forward on that great journey of the soul, in which mortal life is but a single step.

Oftener than once in this inquiry, I have acted towards you like one who, undertaking to guide a traveller through a beautiful valley, should frequently lead him out of the beaten road to climb precipitous eminences, promising that the delay in the accomplishment of the journey should be compensated by the pleasure of extensive prospects over the surrounding region. Conduct like this would be excusable in a guide if the person escorted had leisure for the divergence, and it would be incumbent on him if the acquisition of a knowledge of the country were one of the purposes of the journey; but in either case the labour of the ascents would be recompensed to the traveller, only if the landscapes presented were interesting and distinctly seen. For similar reasons, my endeavour to propose wider views than the subject necessarily suggested has, I conceive, been fully justifiable; but it is for you to decide whether the attempt has been so far successful as to repay your exertions in attending my excursive steps. The first of our lengthened digressions has allowed us to combine the known facts as to the kind and amount of Shakspeare's studies, and to draw from them certain conclusions, which I cannot think altogether valueless, as to some distinctions between him and his dramatic coevals, and as to the source of some peculiarities of his which have been visited with heavy censure. In the second instance in which we have branched off from the main argument, we have been led to reflect on the most characteristic qualities of the poet's mode of thought. If there be any truth or distinctness in the hints which have been imperfectly and hastily thrown out on this head, your own mind will classify, modify, or extend them; and, never forgetting what is the fundamental principle of the great poet's strength, you will regard that essential quality with the more lively admiration, when you discriminate the operations of the power from the working of those other principles which minister to it, and when you remark the number, the variety, the opposition of the mental faculties, which are all thus enlisted under the banners of the one intense and almost philosophical Perception of Dramatic Truth. That stern inquisition into the human heart, which the finest sense of dramatic perfection elevates into the ideal, and the richest fancy touches with poetical repose, will awaken in your mind a softened solemnity of feeling, like that under whose sway we have both wandered in the mountainous forests which skirt our native river; the continuous and gloomy canopy of the gigantic pines hanging overhead like a dungeon roof, while the green sward which was the pavement of the woodland temple, and the lines of natural columns which bounded its retiring avenues, were flooded with the glad illumination of the descending sunset. We reflect with wonder that the most anxious of all poetical inquirers into truth, is also the most powerful painter of unearthly horrors, and the most felicitous creator of romantic or imaginary beauty; that the poet of Richard and Iago is also the poet of Juliet, of Ariel, and of Titania; that the fearfully real self-torture, the judicially inflicted remorse of Macbeth, is set in contrast with the wildest figures which superstitious imagination ever conceived; that on the same canvass on which Hamlet stands as a personification of the Reason of man shaken by the assaults of evil within him and without, the gates of the grave are visibly opened, and the dead ascend to utter strange secrets in the ear of night. But even this union is less extraordinary than the regular and unparalleled consistency with which the poet's faculties early expanded themselves, and the full activity with which through life all continued to work. Even the dramatic soul of Homer ebbed like the sea, sinking in old age into the substitution of wild and minutely told adventure for the historical portraiture of mental grandeur and passionate strength. The youth of Milton brooded over the love and loveliness of external nature; it was not till his maturity of years that he soared into the empyrean or descended sheer into the secrets of the abyss; and advancing age brought weakness with it, and quenched in the morass of polemical disputation the torch which had flamed with sacred light. Shakspeare alone was the same from youth to age; in youth no imperfection, in age no mortality or decay; he performed in his early years every department of the task which he had to perform, and he laboured in it with unexhausted and uncrippled energies till the bowl was broken at the fountain: experience visited him early, fancy lingered with him to the last; the rapid developement of his powers was an indication of the internal strength of his genius; their steady continuance was a type and prognostic of the perpetual endurance of his sway. The cold and fiendish Gloster was an early conception; the eager Shylock and the superhuman Hamlet were imagined simultaneously not long afterwards; the tenderness of Lear was the fruit of the poet's ripest age; and one of the closing years of his life gave birth to the savage wildness and the youthful and aerial beauty of The Tempest.

Our last words are claimed by the proper subject of our inquiry. Have I convinced you that in the composition of The Two Noble Kinsmen, Shakspeare had the extensive participation which I have ascribed to him? It is very probable that my reasoning is in many parts defective; but I place so much confidence in the goodness of the cause itself, that I would unhesitatingly leave the question, without a word of argument, to be determined by any one, possessing a familiar acquaintance with both the poets whose claims are to be balanced, and an ordinarily acute discernment of their distinguishing qualities. I am firmly persuaded that the subject needs only to have attention directed to it; and my investigation of it cannot have been a failure in every particular. The circumstances attending the first publication of the drama do not, in the most unfavourable view which can with any fairness be taken of them, exclude us from deciding the question of Shakspeare's authorship by an examination of the work itself; and it is unnecessary that the effect of the external evidence should be estimated one step higher. Do the internal proofs allot all to Fletcher, or assign any share to Shakspeare? The Story is ill-suited for the dramatic purposes of the one poet, and belongs to a class of subjects at variance with his style of thought, and not elsewhere chosen by him or any author of the school to which he belonged: both the individual and the class accord with the whole temper and all the purposes of the other poet, and the class is one from which he has repeatedly selected themes. It is next to impossible that Fletcher can have selected the subject; it is not unlikely that Shakspeare may have suggested it; and if the execution of the plan shall be thought to evince that he was in any degree connected with the work, we can hardly avoid the conclusion that it was by him that the subject was chosen. The proof here, (which I think has not been noticed by any one before me,) seems to me to be stronger than in any other branch of the argument. The Scenical Arrangement of the drama offers points of resemblance to Shakspeare, which, at the very least, have considerable strength when they are taken together, and are corroborative of other circumstances. The Execution of that large proportion of the drama which has been marked off as his, presents circumstances of likeness to him, so numerous that they cannot possibly have been accidental, and so strikingly characteristic that we cannot conceive them to be the product of imitation. Even if it should be doubted whether Shakspeare chose the subject, or arranged any part of the plot, it seems to me that his claim to the authorship of these individual parts needs only examination to be universally admitted; not that I consider the proof here as stronger than that which establishes his choice of the plot, but because it is of a nature to be more easily and intuitively comprehended.

In forming your opinion, you will be careful to view the circumstances, not singly, but together, and to give each point of resemblance the support of the others. It may be that every consideration suggested may not affect your mind with equal strength of conviction; but numerous probabilities all tending the same way are sufficient to generate positive certainty: and it argues no imperfection in a result that it is brought out only by combined efforts. In those climates of the New World which you have visited, a spacious and lofty chamber receives a diffusive shower of light through a single narrow aperture, while in our cloudy region we can gather sufficient light for our apartments only by opening large and numerous windows: the end is not gained in the latter case without greater exertion than that which is required in the former, but it is attained equally in both; for the aspect of our habitations is not less cheerful than that of yours.

On the absolute merit of the work, I do not wish to anticipate your judgment. So far as Shakspeare's share in it is concerned, it can be regarded as no more than a sketch, which would be seen to great disadvantage beside finished drawings of the same master. Imperfect as it is, however, it would, if it were admitted among Shakspeare's acknowledged works, outshine many, and do discredit to none. It would be no unfair trial to compare it with those works of his in which he abstains from his more profound investigations into human nature, permitting the poetical world actively to mingle with the dramatic, and the radiant spirit of hope to embrace the sterner genius of knowledge. We may call up before us the luxurious fancies of the Midsummer Night's Dream, or even the sylvan landscapes of the Forest of Ardennes, and the pastoral groupes which people it; and we shall gladly acknowledge a similar though harsher style of colouring, and a strength of contour indicating the same origin. But perhaps there is none of his works with which it could be so fairly compared as Henry VIII. In the tone of sentiment and imagination, as well as in other particulars, I perceive many circumstances of likeness, which it will gratify you to trace for yourself. The resemblance is more than a fanciful one, and the neglected play does not materially suffer by the comparison.

This drama will never receive the praise which it merits, till it shall have been admitted among Shakspeare's undoubted works; and, I repeat, it is entitled to insertion if any one of the conclusions to which I have attempted to lead you be sound,—if it be true that he wrote all, or most, or a few, of those portions of it, which more competent judges than I have already confidently ascribed to him. Farewell.

W. S.

Edinburgh, March 1833.

SD - #0036 - 250122 - C0 - 229/152/7 - PB - 9780461737301 - Gloss Lamination